MW01098055

Photo by Maggie Saunders

ROADWORK

ROCK & ROLL TURNED INSIDE OUT

By Tom Wright with Susan VanHecke

Foreword by Pete Townshend

Copyright © 2007 by Tom Wright and Susan VanHecke

All rights reserved. No part of this book may be reproduced in any form, without written permission, except by a newspaper or magazine reviewer who wishes to quote brief passages in connection with a review.

Published in 2007 by
Hal Leonard Books (an imprint of Hal Leonard Corporation)
19 West 21st Street, New York, NY 10010

Printed in United States of America

Book design by Lesley Kunikis

Library of Congress Cataloging-in-Publication Data

Wright, Tom, (Thomas R.), 1944-
  Roadwork : rock & roll turned inside out / by Tom Wright with Susan VanHecke; foreword by Pete Townshend.
     p. cm.
  ISBN-13: 978-1-4234-1300-4
  ISBN-10: 1-4234-1300-8
  1. Rock musicians--Biography. 2. Rock musicians--Travel. 3. Wright, Tom, (Thomas R.), 1944- 4. Photographers—United States--Biography. 5. Photographers—United States—Travel. I. VanHecke, Susan. II. Title.
  ML394.W75 2007
  781.66092--dc22
  [B]
2007006780

www.halleonard.com
www.tomwrightphotography.com

ACKNOWLEDGMENTS

My deepest gratitude to Jodie Rhodes for believing in this project, for connecting me with my co-author, and for turning three decades of "no" into "yes."

To Jan Reed, Ginni and Tony, Lorne Darnell, Roy Flukinger, John Payne, Don Carleton, George Cortez and the Cortez family, Armando, Jesse Trevino, Maggie Saunders, Jim Wright, Oscar Decker, Chris Easter, Dr. Michael Hutchison, Roy Ellison, Royce Deans, Chris Stamp, Joe Walsh, Smokey, Harry Phillips, Larry Lawrence, Tim Bartlett, Cam Bruce, Russ Gibb, Rick Coates, Dodd Russell, Tom Porter, Ian McLagan, Larry Knight, Chaz, Martha Finstamaker, Karen Gavin, Buel Newman, Greg Butler, Darren Atkinson, Danielle Grattage, Lisa Knauf, Chris Laumer, Russ Schlagbaum, John Cerullo, Allison Beck, Dennis Cafferey, Laura Miller, Dave Miller, Steve Voorhies, Geoff Daking, Bill and Betty Perkinson, Patrick Cullie, and the many, many others who kept my spirits up—very special and heartfelt thanks for your support.

— Tom Wright

CONTENTS

Pete Townshend

Tom Wright. Good man. I have always been susceptible to a good man. My first was Graham Beard, my best friend (though I was perhaps not his best) from the age of four until about eleven when we went to watch Bill Haley play and I picked up a guitar. Then I was befriended by an assortment of fellows, from among whom John Entwistle rose as the most constant until I was seventeen. Then at Ealing Art School in the spring of 1962 I met Richard Barnes (later an important Who biographer) and we laughed our way into a long-standing friendship so intense that it's not surprising it has quieted in recent years. Barney and I soon met Tom and ended up in an apartment in the same house he shared with his friend Cam.

Almost as soon as I found Tom, or he found me, I felt I lost him. Tom and Cam were effectively deported from the U.K. for possession of the marijuana that had, along with perfectly faded Levi's and the wonderful collection of R&B records they shared, made them both stars among the prettiest females and the coolest males at the college where Tom studied photography. I read Tom's story in this book and find that he numbers me among the coolest males in 1962. Indeed, I appear to be the coolest in some ways, but I was not cool. I was just susceptible.

Within a few days of hearing Lightning Hopkins mauling out his tortured, primitive version of "Trouble in Mind" I had worked out how to play my own version of it. When Tom heard me play it, he adopted me. Hanging with Tom, as his in-house troubadour, always had a drop-dead moment hanging portentously in the air: the instant he decided to crash into bed to embrace whichever beautiful girl was in his orbit. It would be a few years on before I was able to turn my own best assets into an equally intoxicating bird call.

Music is magical. When they were deported, Tom and Cam had to leave their records behind with Barney and me…as well as their beds. The musical kudos exerted by Tom and Cam were suddenly passed to us. Not necessarily with quite the same romantic association, but we could unleash memories. Tom says in this book that he also left behind a stash of grass. That must have increased our pull, but it also confused my fellows in the Detours, the school band I still played with because it earned so much money. I think I became a little difficult in the months I first began to get stoned. I was hearing music in a new way. The Detours were pretty good, and when I started to introduce some R&B songs into the set during late 1963, the surprise for us

Pete Townshend
Edmonton, Canada, 1967

all was that the audience of Mods who were starting to embed themselves in the local area where we most often performed were fairly in sync with us. Indeed, as I taught John Entwistle "Green Onions" by Booker T. and the MGs, the Rolling Stones were playing their first few shows at the local Ealing Club, casting the first serious glove down to the Beatles, who were already beginning to seem like aliens, they were so successful. By the time Tom and Cam's R&B music collection had been filtered into the Ealing scene, they had been forced to leave the country and watch from afar as the British music revolution took place with R&B as its new backbone.

Tom Wright
Ealing, 1962

It was not until several years later that Tom and I reconnected. He worked on the road with the Who in 1967, and took some of the most flattering photographs of the band ever. I quickly realized Tom had a problem. He liked taking pictures and developing the negatives, but he wasn't crazy about making prints. He wasn't even keen on opening the various trunks in which they were haphazardly stored. So the stash of unseen images grew. Some took thirty years to get printed, some even longer. But whenever any of his friends saw his pictures, we knew he had an extraordinary gift to capture the moment: he seemed to sense the gentle approaching warp in time that predicted that something special would happen. Tom lived so much in the moment, waiting for the moment, that some of us felt he would never properly catalog and archive his work, let alone find time to tell his incredible life story.

His recent successful but substantial heart surgery provided the hiatus, the shock, and finally the focus for this moving, touching, and funny book that tells and illustrates more about the change in the function of pop music from the late '50s to the early '60s than any semi-academic treatise written by journalist or critic. It is clear now that R&B was vital to the shift in function of postwar pop. From dance music designed as a romantic salve for the walking wounded of various wars, we moved to the irritant teenaged codes of '60s pop. This new music was partly aimed at that same scarred older generation and suggested that their postwar trauma, horror, and shame—hitherto denied and untreated—had somehow echoed down to us. R&B, mainly performed by American black musicians and including some powerfully rhythmic jazz and the most edgy folk music of the time, was what underpinned British pop music of the '60s new wave. The combination of complaint, confrontation, and self-healing that was wrapped up in the average R&B song—usually sung by a disgruntled but sanguine older black American—was the right model for my white middle- and working-class British generation too. It changed for the next forty years the purpose and function of pop music itself.

Tom has placed himself inside his own story, and that was necessary. This is also very much my story. There is much of my life that Tom describes that will not appear in my own memoirs simply because I don't remember it. Some of his tales started me laughing, some made me sad. The photographs are all wonderful, providing the context and tangential color that makes Tom's story seem as particular, real, and romantic as it must have felt to him as he experienced it.

One thing is certain, had I not met Tom Wright, the Who would never have become successful. We would have remained the Detours, a solid little pop band doing what hundreds of others were doing around the same time: playing local clubs, pubs, weddings, and parties purely for pleasure and

The Who
1967

fitting the program in and around our day jobs. After a few years I would have stopped playing with them and gone off to work as a sculptor, or for an ad agency. I needed the nudge of marijuana to help me realize I had real creative musical vision. I needed to hear Jimmy Reed to know powerful music could be made with extremely basic tools. I needed to be given the recognition that I got from Tom of my special talent, recognition that Roger Daltrey, the leader of our band, could not give me at first because he had known me and nurtured me before I grew into my real skin.

It's wonderful to be able to say that today I am susceptible to Roger Daltrey. But the memory of meeting Tom in 1962, and being specially blessed by him when he was at his teenage peak, is the most significant moment of my musical life. Roger Daltrey often puts the success of the Who down to his efforts in 1962 of getting me out of bed, where I lay stoned listening to Jimmy Reed, to go and play a local pub show with the Detours. I'm afraid, as is often the case in Who history, Roger and I must differ. I put our success down to the fellow who left that particular bed behind when he was deported.

The Who
1967

INTRODUCTION

This is the tale of two journeys.

The first began in 1960 when my stepfather moved my family to London, I enrolled at Ealing Art College, and there I met Pete Townshend. He was studying graphic design; I was learning photography. I turned him on to American blues and pot. He introduced me to a rock and roll rebirth.

Europeans like Pete saw the '60s and '70s as a full-blown renaissance in music and art. Americans saw it as a revolution. I thought it was both. Even if I was only half-right, I figured my mission was to stay tuned to what was going on and take pictures of the good stuff.

So when Pete's band, the Who, came to the United States in 1967, I joined the tour as a photographer. From then on, I traveled with them as often as I could, whenever they played the States. In 1968 and '69, I managed the Grande Ballroom, flashpoint for the Detroit rock scene that was exploding with raw acts like the MC5, Ted Nugent's Amboy Dukes, and the Stooges. At the Grande, I put on shows and became acquainted with artists like Led Zeppelin, Jeff Beck, Traffic, Steve Miller, and others. It was at the Grande that Pete and the Who performed their landmark rock opera, *Tommy*, for the first time in the United States. As a tour manager, but mostly a freelance photographer, I also worked with the Rolling Stones, Rod Stewart and the Faces, Joe Walsh and the James Gang, and many others.

Joe Walsh (left)
Kent, Ohio, 1969

Rod Stewart (right)
Faces tour, early '70s

For two decades I wore my camera like a gun in a belt. I'd wake up with it around my neck; I didn't want to miss anything by having to turn away to look for it. To me, a new roll of film was like a fresh clip of silver bullets. On the road with rock's best and brightest, I learned that you could actually feel it when you took a good shot. The light. The situation. The balance. It was a matter of everything happening all at once. And you just knew it when you took it. A good photo was like a poem or riff that was just so right you'd never want to forget it. And I couldn't wait to see the negatives. So I figured out how to develop film anywhere—on chartered planes, on tour buses, but mostly in hotel bathrooms that I converted into darkrooms.

Being in the flow was what I liked. The excitement of the '60s and '70s was roaring past us all. We were in the front car of a spaced-out roller coaster, and every once in a while I'd just turn around and snap everybody's picture.

Rod Stewart
Los Angeles, 1972

Tom Wright
2003

I wasn't one of those guys who stopped the roller coaster, rearranged it, made everybody get out and use hair spray. I got the shots from the inside.

It turned out that a lot of the bands I worked with were part of the most influential renaissance in human history, a war waged against things phony and mediocre by artists who were willing to go down in flames in the process. This wasn't about money. It was about taking risks. Making a statement. Telling the truth. And that invisible spirit, that inherent sense of fearlessness, discovery, and experimentation, still hangs in the back of a lot of people's minds, still hovers over their music collections.

I shot the whole thing from within the eye—at least half a million pictures—while the public, the press, and front row photographers were outside blowing in the wind . . . misunderstanding everything. Over the years, they've drummed it into our heads that that era, with its drug-taking and flower-waving longhairs, was boring and stupid. Stupid? Debatable. Boring? No way. The war, the draft, cities on fire, Kent State, new drugs, bad

Tom Wright and Karen with the Rolling Stones and Meteors
San Antonio, 1975

drugs, narcs. Something new and astounding took your breath away every time you switched on the radio. Back then, I just assumed that everyone was drawing the same conclusions as I was. That your family, your school, your hometown cop, your government were all lying through their teeth. That good music could change more things than speeches, politics, and wars. That a lot of musicians were founts of real truth. Pete's "I know you've deceived me, now here's a surprise/I know that you have 'cause there's magic in my eyes"—well, it all made sense. And it was the undeniable truth.

Today, you can create a band at the kitchen table. The deal's already done before the first members show up. It's just an exercise in marketing. The Beatles, Woodstock, Jimi Hendrix—they changed music, changed culture, changed thought. And it all happened so fast, almost at warp speed. Something as simple as "Sunshine of Your Love," and the world wasn't the same. It was as if you couldn't even remember how things were before that song was branded on your brain. The musicians, the fans, the characters I was shooting were laying down track while the train was running, and the more people who got involved, the faster it all went. There was no time to plan where it was going, no time to chart out the course, no time for explanations.

Vancouver, Canada, 1967

I've always wanted to set the record straight. In the '70s, I took an armload of stuff to a giant corporate publishing house and met with a powerhouse editor who kept me running back and forth to his office for more than a week and said he was consulting with his daughter in the Hamptons, who knew about this sort of thing. In the end, it all boiled down to wanting more pictures of debauchery, trashed hotels, and Mick Jagger's lips. And, oh yeah, by the way, rock books don't sell.

Later, I was doing a balancing act, walking the high wire between touring with bands like the Eagles, the Fabulous Thunderbirds, J. D. Souther, and Elvis Costello, and performing my dutiful roles as ex-husband and significant other, father and almost-breadwinner. For me, music, musicians, and life on the road were the normal, understandable things. Marriage, parenthood, and steady paychecks were the psychedelic stuff. Trotting off to shoot a few Rolling Stones or Who dates seemed routine; if a neighbor asked me to photograph his wedding, I'd panic, screw up the film, and then

get embarrassingly drunk at the reception. Rock and roll stories were the only interesting things I could talk about. Problem was, I wasn't interested anymore. And neither were those who'd lived through these moments with me. I just couldn't face telling another Keith Moon tale.

From the late '70s until the early '90s, I was a walking garage sale, moving from one place to another. I wound up doing odd jobs, and if I wasn't asleep, I was drinking. Not just drinking, but revenge drinking: passing out, not wanting to wake up. I was sleeping on the floor of low-rent apartments packed with trunks of my negatives and tapes—dazed, confused, and completely baffled by the significance, or not, of the last twenty-five years. Had I wasted the best decades of my life chasing rock people around the globe? Was my photography garbage? Did it have any meaning? I honestly didn't know.

In 1989, after I'd lost myself in the color and spirit of Texas and Mexico and crawled in and out of rehab with mixed results, I heard that the Who were touring North America. I felt a familiar tug. I couldn't resist. A friend bought me a plane ticket, and I surprised the band in Toronto.

Seeing Pete, Roger, and John at the top of their form, now musically and emotionally mature, true artists, it dawned on me that my work on the road had not been in vain. Now I wished that I'd kept better care of everything during all those years I'd lost to depression and self-doubt. Now I realized that had Townshend and I not met, there may have never been a Who so grounded in blues; there may never have been a Tom Wright, photo-guy. Both of our lives were changed drastically by meeting each other—and therein lays a microcosm of the era. Nitro was splashed on glycerin all those years ago, and people's lives and new dreams were exploding all over the place . . . all over the world. As a witness to that rock renaissance, that rock revolution, I was a sort of custodian of cultural and social history. And it was my duty to get it all down.

So the decision to write this book was the start of a second journey, one that put me back on the road, reexamining formative experiences and reexploring old relationships. I'd survived the takeoff and was now settling into orbit. Maybe I could finally put things into perspective.

Age helps in flattening out the past. For me, looking back is like staring at my own X-rays and seeing what's been there all along, hidden beneath the surface. Of course it's important, but what does it all mean? I could use a second opinion.

James Gang and friends
after Rides Again shoot

CHAPTER TWO

Who Are You?

Clearwater, Florida. 1967. I was last in line as we climbed up the steel stairway to the open door at the front of the plane. I moved slowly, wanting to remember everything. I breathed in deeply through my nose, trying to hold the sensation. I could smell the aircraft—whiffs of cooked, clean metal, diesel fuel, a hint of rubber. The scent of Florida overpowered it all, though, that heavy, humid air that's part expectant rain, part sea breeze, part citrus fresh.

Five years had passed since Pete and I had been together at Ealing. In the fall of '62, I was busted for pot and asked by the courts to leave immediately. They didn't even give me time to collect my belongings. I ended up giving my Fender guitar, record collection, and the stash of marijuana they didn't find to Pete.

I went to Paris first, where I took photos of writers and poets for book cover jackets and then printed them on postcards to sell. After a year, I left for Ibiza in the Balearic Islands off the coast of Spain. When my parents moved back to Florida, I returned to their home and scored a job—my first real one—as an underwater photographer. Low-key, kinda boring, and very legit.

Then everything changed in '67 when I heard a Who song, "Happy Jack," on the radio. I didn't know it was the Who at first, but I recognized Pete's voice at the very end of the song. "I sar ya!" he shouted as the music stopped. I sent Pete a letter to congratulate him on his new record.

He telegrammed back that the Who were coming to the U.S. to tour with the British pop band Herman's Hermits, along with American psychedelic rockers the Blues Magoos. They'd be in Florida in a week or so and I should come to the show, the telegram urged. When I got there, Pete suggested I come on tour with them and shoot photos of the band.

And so here I was, twenty-three years old, camera around my neck, passport in my back pocket, boarding a chartered plane because Herman's Hermits were so big they rated it.

The Who
1967

By the time I'd made it from the runway into the plane, I'd reviewed my whole life. Especially the parts when I'd been on my own. My feeling, as I sank into a window seat, was that I'd proven I could get a real job, settle down, and stick with things—if only for three months.

Now I was leaving town in a plane that'd seen better days, loaded with English musicians. Somehow it seemed more natural than punching a clock, putting on a wetsuit, and planning for lunch.

I was on the road with the Who.

Pete introduced me to the group. There was Roger Daltrey, who looked just as he had onstage in St. Petersburg the night before, like he was balancing a few loose grapes on top of an elaborate hat we couldn't see. John Entwistle, done up like he was going to the prom: black vest with a ruffled shirt, black suit jacket thrown on the seat next to him. And Keith Moon, curled up on a set of seats, a Holiday Inn bedspread flung over him. He stuck out his hand, said, "Cheers!" as he shook mine, and then disappeared back under the covers.

Then Pete introduced me to the headliners, Herman's Hermits, and the Blues Magoos, who were, like Pete's band, an opener. I remember feeling sorry for Herman's Hermits at the show in St. Pete. I was sure that after the Who's set everyone would have to leave, things had gone so badly—Pete banging his guitar, splinters flying everywhere. The music was so loud it had felt like we were standing inside a jet engine. Surely it was the end of Pete, the end of concerts in Florida, I'd thought. A deejay at the side of the stage, his eyes wide, ears ringing, could only mumble, "Wow, wow, wow," over and over. The audience didn't know if they liked it or not. They'd come to see Herman, but they'd gotten bulldozed in the face by the Who.

The inside of the plane reminded me of an old car: it had a musty, worn upholstery feel. Pete sat down next to me. A guy in jeans and a denim shirt shut the door, locked it, double-checked it.

"Brian, the stewardess," Pete told me. "Also the flight mechanic. Nice bloke."

I took that as a good omen. After all, if the flight mechanic was onboard, I reasoned, he had something to lose, too.

The engines cranked up one at a time and we started taxiing toward the main runway at the Clearwater airport. The only runway, actually. It didn't look like there was any commercial airliner traffic at the tiny facility anymore, just a lot of single-engine private planes. We were in a well-worn, unmarked prop job, rolling toward the end of the runway for takeoff, looking, I'm sure, a little too big for our britches.

When we reached the runway's end, the plane whirled around, the brakes locked, and the pilots revved the engines to full blast. Ready. I stared at the grass growing at the edge of the runway. The pilots released the brakes and we started to roll. The grass blurred as we accelerated.

Just then I saw the front fender of a Ford station wagon. I couldn't believe my eyes. It was chasing us down the runway.

"Pete, check this out," I said with a bemused chuckle. "There's a guy out there racing us."

Keith Moon
1968

By the time Pete unbuckled and leaned over to peer out, we could see the driver. He was bouncing along, yelling and shooting us the finger. Pete laughed. I returned the guy's favor, sticking my upright finger against the window. We must have been doing eighty when the driver produced a double-barreled shotgun. He pointed it at the plane and fired twice. Flames leapt from the muzzle. Pete and I jumped back from the window as the plane left the ground, lofting us to safety.

I'd just departed Florida in a dilapidated, four-engine prop plane that some nut was using for target practice. And this was just my first ten minutes on tour with the Who.

An hour later, we landed in Jackson, Mississippi. No one, including me, had ever heard of the place. The whole planeload, including the pilots, checked into a Holiday Inn. That was pretty upscale in those days, especially compared to the humble English digs these musician guys had probably grown up in, or the cramped London flats they shared after leaving home to be in a band.

Keith Moon
Jackson, Mississippi, 1967

For the rest of that first day, the band stayed indoors and watched television. The English guys still couldn't get over the fact that American TV was on all the time and that there were three stations. In England, you just had the BBC, which was off the air by 11:30 PM each night.

On the plane, Pete had formally announced to the band that I would be taking group shots the following day. They were to bring or wear their stage clothes, he'd instructed.

This was the photo shoot that I'd left home for. This was serious. Hell, I'd even brought two cameras, my Rolleiflex and my Nikon. So I talked the college kid who drove the Holiday Inn courtesy van into driving me around Jackson so I could scout a place for the shoot. There was nothing much downtown, just some old brick buildings and a lot of old cars. The few locals around stared at the hotel van like it was a UFO. Eventually, the

kid found the road out of town. I was hopeful I could find some place that didn't scream American South.

Just past the city limit sign, parked off of the side of the road, the kid and I came across a house trailer. The folks inside were selling fireworks. I bought two boxes of smoke bombs and on the way back to town picked up four rolls of black-and-white film at a drugstore. I was set. I went back to the Holiday Inn and drank with the Herman's Hermits guys until the bar closed.

The next day, the band was awake at the crack of noon, and by two o'clock we were all loaded into a rental station wagon the hotel had arranged for us. I was the only one with a valid driver's license. I pretended to know where I was going.

The summer afternoon light was good—or at least interesting. It had

Roger Daltrey
Jackson, Mississippi, 1967

clouded over and looked like it was going to rain. Occasionally the sun would break through and great golden shafts would stream down for brief moments. The weather was warm, without a breeze.

When I finally found what looked vaguely like an English meadow, with no buildings, cows, or rows of cotton, I turned off onto a dirt road. The band got out and donned their stage jackets—blazing bright patterns that didn't go together. Their fashions were made from flags from the British Isles; Pete's Union Jack was the only one I recognized. Standing alone, they all looked fine; side-by-side, though, it was way out of sync, jolting and electric. Nobody would be mistaking the Who for the cookie-cutter Beatles. But maybe that's what they wanted. More than likely they didn't think about it much.

Except for Pete, I didn't really know anybody in the band, but the attempted assassination of the day before now gave us something in common to talk about. Turns out, Moon had slept with an underage girl the night before takeoff. We decided that the odds were pretty good it was her irate father driving the chase car.

I started the session with individual portraits. Roger was ready as soon as he got out of the car. As the lead singer, he acted as if I'd want to photograph him first, so I did. He was a little stiff and shy and, through the camera lens, came off like an Edwardian rich kid with big hair—and a Cockney accent.

After spending about ten minutes with each guy, I lined up the band and set up my tripod in front of them. With my cigarette, I lit as many smoke bombs as I could hold in my right hand and then tossed them, all at once, behind the band then ran back to the camera. I could get two or three shots before the haze, stinking of smoldering garbage and wet firecracker fuses, drifted away.

Swirling rainbows of colored smoke billowed behind the band, mere puffs compared to the stuff they filled the auditorium with closing their show the day before. In their clashing flag jackets, they stood out against the gray clouds and rolling meadows of Mississippi, looking all the world like thugs in a lineup. The Stones looked sneaky and illegal in their pictures, too, but the Who looked like they were daring me to do something about it, daring me to finger them for their crime. They were proud of something, but after the Florida show, I wasn't quite sure what.

When I ran out of smoke bombs and film, we headed for the car. Up the hill, about 200 yards from the station wagon, someone was running toward us with a stick—or maybe it was a gun. We couldn't tell. The band dove into the back seats, I spun the car around, and we flew down the dirt road with the rabid farmer quickly disappearing in swirling clouds of dust. We laughed all the way back to town.

That night, at the Mississippi State Coliseum in Jackson, was my chance to get a group shot onstage. Chris Stamp, the Who's manager, had phoned from London and told me that he was set with pictures of Pete and Roger and that what he really needed was 8x10 black-and-white shots of the whole band. Everyone had to be visible.

As the house lights came up after the Blues Magoos' thirty-minute opening set, the tour manager, an older guy in a suit who was responsible for everything, took me out in front of the stage. He held up a velvet rope marking a large semicircle in front of the stage. Every six feet, Mississippi state troopers lined the outside of the circle, as if protecting the rope. They stood facing the crowd, decked out in dark brown cowboy hats, holstered guns, sticks, and long black flashlights.

I started shooting as the Who came on. The light here was better than the bluish dim of the St. Petersburg show, more like the emergency-crew glare at a car wreck. The band banged away, but the audience didn't much care, everyone talking to each other, chewing gum, bouncing up and down, anxiously awaiting Mrs. Brown's lovely whatever.

To get all of the Who in the frame, I had to keep backing up. Eventually, I ducked under the rope. I got about ten group shots, then headed back under the rope toward the stage.

The Who
Jackson, Mississippi, 1967

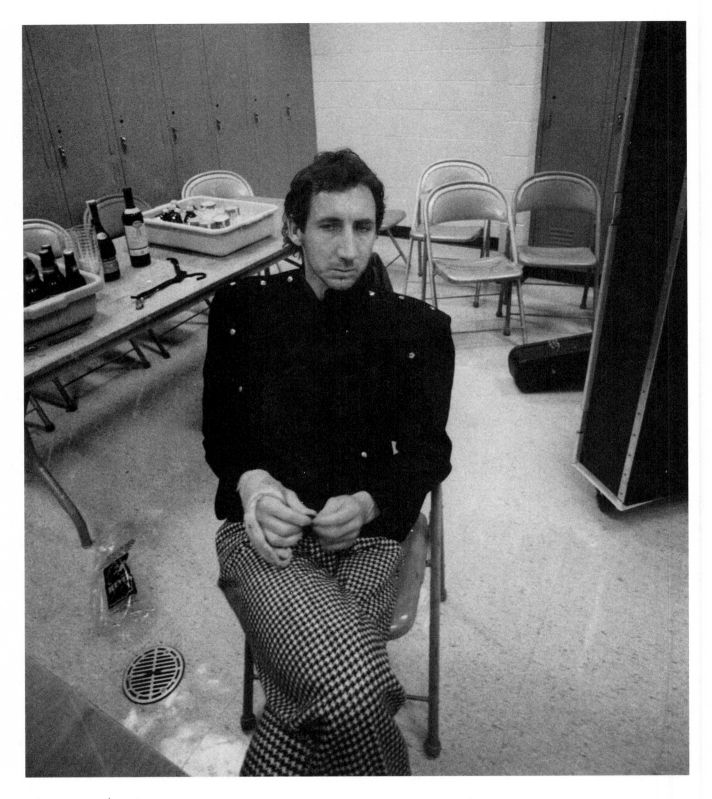

Pete Townshend
Baton Rouge, Louisiana, 1982

That's when several of those long black flashlights apparently landed full-force on the back of my head. Next thing I remember I was coming to, my head atilt, and the side of my face pressed flat up against the wet, warm pavement. As my lids lifted, I felt like I'd just been born. At that moment, life seemed wondrous and simple. I didn't want to move.

It was raining. Except for a single light hanging over the worn metal door in front of me, it was pitch black. The rain and the wet sparkled and glistened. I could feel my heart beating, steady, calm. I lay there for no more than a minute or so—my reintroduction to the world. Blinking my eyes, breathing, I was in heaven. I was sure of it, even though the door read "NO ADMITTANCE" upside down and backwards.

When I sat up, I realized I was wet and slimy. My camera was soaked. I could hear the band churning out "My Generation," the last song of their set. I stood up and banged on the metal door as hard as I could, but it didn't seem to make much of a noise. The back of my head was throbbing. Blood slithered down my neck. I stumbled around to the front of the building. Two Mississippi police officers stopped me in my tracks.

"You can't come in!" one of them barked.

"Show's over!" said the other.

"Yes, I know," I said, trying to focus. "I'm with the band."

"They already left," said the first cop. "Go around to the back." He put his hand down on his nightstick like he was about to shift into second.

"Thanks," I mumbled, too dazed to realize that it was probably one of these bull-neck troopers who'd cracked me on the head and rolled me into the alley.

Though people were streaming out of the front door, the show was not over. The Who's set was over, but Herman's Hermits were yet to go on. The smashed equipment, the smoke, the photographer getting beat up and tossed out the side door had spooked the audience. The kids pouring out of the building looked like they were fleeing a burning house.

I staggered back to the rear of the coliseum, where a janitor in blue coveralls let me in. The stage curtains were closed, the stage work lights cut through the thick smoke like a lighthouse sweep. That burnt-match smell unique to homemade English smoke bombs stung my nostrils. This was hell, obviously, with still more Mississippi cops wading through the haze.

I was wet, out of breath, bleeding. Everyone milling about backstage was also panting—musicians, stagehands, even the cops.

Searching for Pete, I was pissed. I wanted to tell him off, tell him I'd quit my first real job to do him and his band a favor and now look what had happened. I finally found him sitting alone in Herman's Hermits' dressing room, the only room with a sink, a Holiday Inn bath towel wrapped around his right hand. He looked pale. Blood was everywhere.

"It won't stop," he said, looking up at me. He asked why I was bleeding.

"Banged on the head, just a nick," I said, concern tamping out anger in a heartbeat. "Jesus Christ, Pete, you look like you're bleeding to death!"

The show's promoter let me borrow his car to get Pete to the local hospital. We were the only patients in the waiting room. They took Pete in immediately. I followed along. The doctor arrived, frowning over his clipboard—Dr. Billy Walters, surely not a day over thirty.

"What seems to be the problem?" he asked, washing his hands.

"It's my finger," Pete said politely. "I cut it on my guitar string."

"Are you part of that Herman's Hermit group over at the Coliseum tonight?" He motioned for Pete to unwrap the towel.

"We have our own group," Pete explained. "There's two other groups besides Herman's. I'm with the Who."

Pete held out his finger like he was passing the doctor an imaginary tray of biscuits.

"The Who Is It?" the doctor asked, and then corrected himself. "Oh, just the 'Who'? That's your name?" He looked puzzled and disappointed.

He examined Pete's finger under the light, and then gently held it under the running water.

"You've sliced it to the bone," he said. "It's going to take stitches."

Pete and the doctor stared at each other like somebody was supposed to say something.

"It's tough skin at the end of your finger," the doctor finally said. "And it looks like you've got some scar tissue lumps around there that's tougher still. We'll need to bind your hand down so you don't jerk the needle and do more damage."

He rolled over a little table with leather straps attached to the sides.

"Does this happen a lot in your line of work?" the doctor asked as he adjusted the light and the table height then strapped Pete's arm down, tight.

Dr. Walters spent more than an hour working with a curved needle that looked like a large fishhook. He punctured the skin excruciatingly slowly. Minutes were spent on each hole, until the needle would sort of punch through the skin. Pete bounced his knees under the table as he winced.

When the young doctor was finished sewing and swabbing, Pete's finger resembled a boiled sausage, its swelling insides held back with thick black twine, ugly knots on both sides of each stitch.

"You won't be able to play for at least a month," the doctor told Pete. "Six weeks to be on the safe side."

"It's not like I can stop playing," Pete said. "We're on a tour."

"I'm sorry," said the doctor, "but if you don't let it heal you could lose your finger. Or part of it, anyway."

He packed a bag full of gauze and supplies and handed it to Pete.

"Don't get it wet. And put on new bandages every twenty-four hours."

He gave Pete a clean hand towel then finished up with a tetanus shot.

We headed back to the Holiday Inn, driving through what looked like a suburb of East Berlin in the drizzle. Pete sat quietly in the passenger seat, his right hand bandaged and palm-up on a towel across his leg. He frowned. I kept quiet. Must be wondering how to tell his mum he's coming home, I thought, how to tell the band it's finished.

At the hotel, he got out of the car and stuck his bandage toward me.

"Guess I'll have to glue me pick to the bandage."

I laughed. So it wasn't over. It was just the beginning.

Faces
1972

CHAPTER THREE

Tea with Pete

For old time's sake, the Who Convention in April 2006, was held at Bush Hall, an old dancehall where the band had played some of their earliest gigs. Bush Hall is in Shepherd's Bush, an area of West London that was once their regular stomping ground. In the '50s and '60s, Shepherd's Bush was working-class white. Today it's pan-global, with an emphasis on the Mideast. Afghans, Arabs, Africans, and Pakistanis make up 85 percent of the population, which works out to about 100 percent foreign on the sidewalk. There's now a mosque next to Bush Hall; during noon prayers, facing Mecca, a guy with a microphone was auctioning off a pair of Entwistle shoes next door.

I knew Pete wasn't gonna be there. The Wholigans would be in for soundcheck. That, and to look around, was all I wanted. So I hung around until Andy Neil—co-writer of *Anyway Anyhow Anywhere*, the best Who book ever—showed up, and then the two of us grabbed dinner at an Indian restaurant across the street. We learned later that as we were munching away on prawns and yellow rice, Roger Daltrey had pulled up in an SUV limo, slipped in the back door, jumped on stage with Simon Townshend, Pete's brother, and sang a couple of Who songs, "Behind Blue Eyes" and "Substitute." Then Daltrey thanked everyone for coming, dashed out the back, and rolled off just as Andy and I were finishing our mint tea.

Back at Bush Hall, Keith Moon's mum arrived with half a dozen of Moon's young nieces and cousins in tow and sat at Keith's "Pictures of Lily" reproduction drum kit up in the balcony for a photo op that lasted less than five minutes.

Andy and I wandered outside and found a pub. Over a few pints, he explained that he had a friend who was making a film on Iggy Pop, and that this friend wanted to interview me about the Grande, a nightclub I managed in Detroit back in the late '60s, and what sort of impact Iggy had made there.

A ridiculous subject and a ridiculous premise, but I agreed to do it. It was two days off—what the hell?

Ron Wood
Faces tour plane, mid-'70s

Pete and I got together the day between the convention and the Iggy interview. He said to come by Eel Pie Studios, his office and recording complex, around ten, so I'd been up since five, packing and repacking my shoulder bag, putting new batteries in the handheld recorder, fresh film in the Nikon, a full charge in the digital.

At two minutes to ten, the cab stopped in front of Eel Pie. As I grabbed my bag and wallet, a smiling kid, early twenties, strode up the sidewalk, a bunch of pastries in his hands. "You must be Tom," he said. "Pete's expecting you."

I followed the kid to the side door. He wasn't even born the last time I was here. Now, like a little Indian boy leading a wrinkled old ox from the rice paddy to the shed, he ushered me into the reception area . . . to two other old oxen I'd seen off and on most of my life.

Sitting on the leather couch, reading a worn copy of *Billboard*, was Alan Rogan, Pete's longtime roly-poly guitar tech. He looked up, surprised to see me. The digital camera that hung around my neck—about the size of a thick stage pass, the only digital I could ever operate—was one that he'd given me at our last meeting four years earlier. And standing by the coffee pot was Bob Pridden, Who roadie since 1961, looking exactly like Ben Franklin—bald head ringed with short, white hair, small wire glasses balanced on his nose. Pridden's never missed a gig, he'll proudly tell you after he's known you awhile.

Brian, the kid, left to announce my arrival to Pete.

I settled on the couch next to Alan and asked him if he was still working with the Eagles. "No thanks," he said. "They suddenly wanted me to fly economy everywhere and I took it as the slap in the face that it was." His voice fell to a whisper as something caught his eye in the magazine.

"They've almost finished a Who album," Bob said, retrieving the beat from where Alan dropped it. "And it's bloody well amazing."

Brian returned. "Pete wants you to come up," he chirped. This was fast for rock and roll. This was fast even for the dentist's office.

I followed him into the inner sanctum, around a curved, white wall more than twenty feet long, spotless and empty but for one framed, 20x24 sepia-toned photo of Entwistle right in the middle of the curve, eye level. It was mine. I'd taken it in the States in a dressing room somewhere. Townshend must've bought the print at Christie's. John looked great, cigarette in his mouth, smiling, bass slung over his shoulder. He looked happy and excited, a twinkle in his eyes, a peak moment of his life now the perfect punctuation mark on this pristine wall. A memorial.

Up a flight of stairs and there was Pete, in jeans and a long-sleeve T-shirt, looking like he hadn't been up long. After our customary bear hug, he offered me a cup of tea. I followed him to his office kitchen, which was just big enough for an electric water pot and a sink. Pete poured the boiling water into a large teapot.

I'd expected to find a miserable Pete, since I'd heard that Zak Starkey—Ringo Starr's son, protégé of "Uncle Keith" Moon, and most recent Who drummer—had left for some younger, hipper band. I'd even brought some

John Entwistle
photo hanging at Eel Pie offices
late '70s

old lyrics along on the trip, plus a new song I'd been working on, "Step Twins," thinking Pete might be needing some material. I'd always thought of Pete and Roger as step twins, co-dependent, a love-hate habit. Like a tattoo, stuck for life. I was even prepared to suggest Pete consider Darren, the Wholigans drummer, fill in.

Instead, Pete was bursting with enthusiasm and good cheer and was quick to set me straight. "No, no, no, Zak didn't go anywhere. He's on the tour and he's on the record. All over it." He took a sip of tea. "I finished my Internet novel that you hated, and as soon as I finished it, all I wanted to do was write new Who songs. I could hear them in my mind. Not Pete Townshend songs, mind you, but new Who songs. It's going good. We have about six tracks done and six to go. And Zak is all over it."

I followed Pete to the next room, floor-to-ceiling glass at one end with a long table running down the middle. We sat across from each other and looked out at the River Thames below. Robin Hood and his men could've been gathering on the bank across the water and not looked the least bit out of place. The tea was good. It was English, Pete had made it, it was the way he drank it.

Rogan has said that within the first second of seeing Pete on any given day, he can tell if everything's wrong or everything's okay just by the look on Pete's face. Here at the table, shut off from everything but memories and the view, his mood was up. He smiled easily, seemed totally happy. For forty minutes we talked about everything from our flat at Sunnyside Road in '62 to the "Who's Left" tour that would start in a month. There seemed no reason to suggest Darren now. And to pull out old song lyrics or a camera would've been awkward.

"When this tour is finished you should come back," Pete told me. "We can work on your projects here in the studio. We could do recording, we could do film editing, we could do a radio show. I could help you with the book."

It wasn't the first time Pete had wanted to help. Back in the early '80s, after I'd emerged from rehab, I'd struggled with putting a photo book together. Just pictures, hardly any words. I'd asked Pete if he'd write something about my work that would make a potential publisher take a serious look, and he wound up penning a two-page foreword. It looked really cool to me and I showed it around for a while, but then I got caught up with a few more tours and eventually it grew stale in one of my cardboard storage boxes.

Now I could hardly believe what I was hearing. What could be more enjoyable, more productive, than working with Pete? All I could do was stare out the window.

We watched a metal barge making a turn up the river bend, two old guys staring at a painting in motion. Pete grew thoughtful.

"Do you know what we were really doing sitting around Sunnyside getting stoned, listening to Jimmy Reed albums until we'd memorized every note and scratch? We were meditating. Yeah, that was meditation in its deepest sense, in that I can recall it at will all these years later. 'Green Onions'—do you realize how many times we played that record?"

Pete Townshend
Plaza Hotel, New York City
1982

edge of the pool and splattered himself to death. A roadie and a Holiday Inn maintenance guy pulled him out and then hooked the Samsonite with a pool brush. Everything Keith owned was soaked, including the passport in his back pocket.

I have no idea what possessed him to leap. For those who saw it—especially those lounging poolside—Keith Moon's arrival in Nashville was a heart-stopper.

Pete Townshend and Keith Moon
after emergency landing
1967

CHAPTER FIVE

Ealing

We had a couple of days off in Nashville so I had time to set up a makeshift darkroom in my motel bathroom. I assembled my enlarger, changed all the light bulbs in my room to red safelights, taped and tacked blankets over the windows. I needed bottles to mix my chemicals in. Gallon chemical bottles from the camera shop were eight dollars apiece; a gallon of red wine from the liquor store was six bucks. I shelled out eighteen bucks for three gallons of Chianti. My stainless steel developing trays were too big to fit in a footlocker, so I had to improvise. I soon discovered that motel desk and dresser drawers lined with a few thirty-gallon trash bags worked just fine.

The second night, the phone rang. It was Mel, the tour manager. He'd never spoken more than two words to me since I'd been on the road with the band. "Tommy? I was wondering if you might be interested in some company," he said. "I know some people here in Nashville. Professional people. Beautiful people, in fact. The one I'm thinking about for you was here yesterday. Maybe you saw her at the pool?" I did. I was all ears. "Now, she can stop by for about twenty-five dollars. Or she can hang around for an hour for fifty dollars. Anyway, if you're interested, just drop the money down in my room. I'll be here for another hour. There's still a few guys I haven't called yet, but she won't be around very much longer."

I'd already grabbed my wallet and was out the door.

A half-hour later, this low-key hillbilly chick with extra-long brown hair wearing a fringe jacket and almost-but-not-quite miniskirt came in and sat down on one of the beds. She was beautiful, in a white-trash kind of way: bubble gum, cleavage, high heels. You just knew she wasn't the babysitter. I shut the door. Everything went red—red lights; red lips; red wine, a gallon and a half left on the dresser.

"You sure went to a lot of trouble for an hour," she drawled. She lit a cigarette and looked like she was gonna hold a press conference.

"You wanna matchbox?" she asked, slowly licking her lips.

Matchbox? What the hell was that—some kinky country decadence beyond my comprehension? I was speechless . . . but eager.

"Weed," she said, leaning toward me. She blew a smoke ring and a bubble at the same time, then popped the pink orb with her tongue. From

*It always rains on
Sunnyside Road*

the leather purse that hung from her neck, she pulled out a tiny matchbox. She shook it silently. "I've got three left," she said. "Ten bucks each, or three for twenty-five."

"Sold," I said, reaching for my wallet. If this mountain princess was a narc, I was ready to give up and go to jail right now. After the fastest hour I can remember, she left me—thin wallet and all.

I took a quick shower to avoid the clap, and set out to find a store that sold tobacco. I bought a bag of Bull Durham with cigarette papers then called Pete.

"Hey, bring a guitar to 212, I've got something for you."

"Can't come right now," he said, "got someone dropping by. I'll be there later. What is it?"

"I can't tell you," I said. You always assumed that the geek at the switchboard was listening to all the calls, plus I wanted to surprise Pete. I finished off the second gallon of wine and fell asleep watching *Bonanza*.

I woke up to loud banging on the door. "We know you're in there!" someone was shouting.

Pete. I opened the door. He walked into the room, still ablaze in red light.

"Sunnyside," he said in astonishment. "It's Sunnyside all over again!"

We shut the door on the night. He broke out an acoustic guitar. I broke out the matchbox.

The flat at Sunnyside. That's where I first turned Pete on to pot and American blues. Ealing, London, England, 1962.

Three years earlier, when I was sixteen, my stepfather had made the casual dinnertime announcement that, after two years as a civilian, he'd reenlisted in the Air Force, they'd made him a captain, and we were selling the house in Florida and moving to London. It hit me in the gut like a lead medicine ball. I stopped chewing. I stopped breathing. At sixteen, life was to begin. Driver's license, car, sex—the sky was the limit and I was almost there. And now we were packing up and kissing it all good-bye.

England was the coldest, wettest, grayest place I'd ever been. I couldn't

Pete Townshend
Jackson, Mississippi, 1967

figure how people could stand it. And white. The English were so white they were really pale blue. And formal. It looked like everyone was dressed for a funeral that no one could find. Guys my age wore ties, even to school. And the girls—all the girls—wore high heels; they looked like they were playing dress-up.

People in England were so polite I naturally assumed that they were shy, or probably sad, since it was always raining. I began to miss the sound of people laughing out loud. English people spoke in hushed tones and always ended their sentences with "please": "two biscuits, *please*," "one ticket to Hanger Lane, *please*." And the eternal question, the only one that mattered,

*Ealing
1962*

was *"Would you like a cup of tea?"* The pat answer, the proper English answer, was, of course, "Yes, *please*." My American "No, thanks" earned me nothing but scowls and disbelief.

I attended the American school in London and, through a friend there, was introduced to Tim Bartlett, the first English kid I'd ever met. Tim was my age and already in college at nearby Ealing Art School. Fifteen in England was the magic age, Tim explained; you could marry, quit school, join the army, or go to college. Tim showed me just how stuff worked in England— practical stuff, like how to ride the "tubes," the London subway system; when the pubs opened and what to ask for; the ins and outs of British humor. He was far more educational, and a million times more fun, than anyone and anything going on at the high school.

Tim, in fact, was the coolest guy I'd ever met. He wore American Levi's and an American flight jacket with a fur collar; not the leather kind, but that sort of pale avocado green, silky, puffy kind of jacket. It looked warm and worn, and went with jeans and any shirt perfectly. He had long hair that he never touched, and it always seemed just right for every occasion. If the wind blew, it blew; if it rained, it got wet. He looked good all the time.

I learned that a "haircut" in England was something altogether different than in the States. When Americans got a haircut, shears and razors were involved, nothing was to be left touching the ear, and at the end you got sprinkled and rubbed with Aqua Velva that burned all your fresh cuts and nicks, and for the rest of the day you smelled like a Marseilles whore trying to come out of retirement. When the English got a haircut, they called it a "trim." Barbers used scissors only, and they would thatch and shape your hair so it made the rest of your head make sense, kind of like arranging a cloth on a dresser. When you walked out of the shop, you looked good, not like you'd just been sheared for trying to have illicit sex with some perfumed old hooker in Marseilles.

Tim was my guide to the English and their way of life. The more I hung out with him, the more comfortable I felt being in England. After a while, I didn't really care that a couple of slices of cucumber between buttered white bread was called a sandwich, or that a bath was something you took only on the weekends. I didn't worry anymore that no one had a car in England, and that no one had a driver's license because you had to be eighteen to drive. Fact is, you could walk into a bar and buy a beer and no one batted an eye. You could buy cigarettes. You could smoke in school. You could do a lot of stuff that you just couldn't do back in the States.

Nor did I worry that there was never anything on the radio that even vaguely resembled good music, except for one hour on Sundays when you might hear Cliff Richard, the English version of Elvis, or Lonnie Donegan, the king of skiffle, the jazz- and blues-tinged folk music so popular there at the time. Everything else was big band, World War II–sounding stuff, with no guitars. It didn't matter, because Tim had some records. He also had a guitar, a battered acoustic he'd spray-painted white and onto which he'd stenciled his name in four-inch letters.

In 1960, an American LP cost about three dollars in the U.S., and about a dollar at the PX on base in London. In an English record shop, the same album would cost five pounds, or fifteen dollars.

Friday and Saturday nights, Tim worked at a pub carrying ice and cleaning up; he'd save his dough and blow it on records. Seemed nobody in England had records but Tim. When I first met him, he had a small but lively collection, ten or fifteen records. What was amazing, though, was

*Cam in London
1962*

that he handled them so carefully. He had a special cloth he used to wipe the records before and *after* he played them, and all his records went back into their paper sleeves before going in the covers. It blew my mind that he was so thoughtful with something that was so disposable back home. In England, records weren't easily replaced. They were like cars. You couldn't drive them, you couldn't afford them, so eventually you just didn't think about them. Except for Tim.

The word for record player in England was "gramophone." Gramophones played gramophone records. It was a very serious business, above most people's heads and incomes. Tim liked American folk records and thought Big Bill Broonzy and Leadbelly were the greatest things America had ever produced. Well, besides jeans. I had never heard of these people, but I liked them as soon as Tim played them for me, just as Tim had never heard of Jimmy Reed, but dug his music the moment I played it for him.

Tim had a few EPs the size of 45s that played at 33⅓, one from an English band called the Shadows. They were Cliff Richard's backup band, but this was their own record. All-instrumental, kind of Duane Eddy-ish, but they looked so much cooler and had red guitars. He had a couple of Acker Bilk traditional jazz records and Lonnie Donegan. Tim's father owned a gramophone, and if no one was at home, we'd play records. Tim would strum along on his white guitar, figuring out chords. Chords were so complicated, I thought, so many fingers involved.

My other closest friend in England was Cambel, a fellow American I'd met at school. Cam had movie-star looks and money to burn. He owned an expensive Martin guitar that he could play, plus he could sing and wasn't shy about it. He also owned a pristine record collection: every Buddy Holly, every Chuck Berry. His family had come to London from Tulsa; his dad was in the oil business and loaded. I still remember seeing the cover of his school annual from back home, a shot of the school parking lot. There must've been 100 motorcycles and motor scooters, plus Corvettes, Thunderbirds, and convertibles, all gleaming in the sun. James Dean heaven. For his sixteenth birthday, Cam had gotten a brand-new Chevy that he picked out himself. For now, it was in storage back in Tulsa.

Cambel lived in downtown London, and several times a week he'd ride home on the bus with me to our house in Ealing. He and I both loved to drink, and since he never ran out of money, we always hit the pubs. I'd buy him Camel cigarettes by the carton at the base for less than two dollars; he'd buy my pints at the pubs. If Tim was working, we'd go to his pub, play darts, and get buzzed. If Tim wasn't working, the three of us would sit around and play guitar and sing. The best place to do this was at the Ealing water reservoir. It was the size of a soccer stadium, all brick and stone, but never had any water in it. Weather permitting, we'd stand in the middle and sing Everly Brothers tunes and drink strong apple cider 'til we were all too drunk to think. The echo from that spot was epic, and the blending of our voices with the right amount of alcohol sounded just like a record.

On weekends, sometimes we went to the Ealing Club, a tiny basement jazz spot directly across the street from the Ealing tube station. Inside, it looked like Hitler's war room in the Berlin bunker, but with red lights and lots of girls trying to look like Twiggy. It was five shillings to get in, and we'd only go if we liked the band. Our hands-down favorite was Cyril Davies All-Stars. Cyril was an English harmonica player and singer who thought he was an American from Chicago. He wore a little cap like a 1920s newsboy. We all assumed he was bald; he looked old enough. He'd stand right at the front of the stage—wouldn't look at the audience, wouldn't look at the band, never said a thing—and belt out every song Muddy Waters had ever recorded, plus Jimmy Reed, Little Walter, and Howlin' Wolf. And he was as good as it got. You could tell he was stoned, you could tell he was great, you could tell everything about him except that he was English. Every song, he just nailed it. Cam, Tim, and I all agreed that if Muddy Waters were playing next door, we'd still be there with Cyril Davies. Cyril died onstage in '64 at another blues club in West London. I heard he suffered a brain hemorrhage in the middle of a song and fell face first onto a cement floor. What a way to go.

The other band worth five shillings was Alexis Korner's Blues Incorporated. Members varied, at times including Jack Bruce, Charlie Watts, Ginger Baker,

Pete Townshend
stoned at Sid's Cafe, 1962

and other future greats. Korner was the white godfather of British blues, and for the young guys, playing in his band was like going to blues school. He knew everything, sat on a bar stool with an electric guitar that took over the room, and would play every blues tune you could possibly think of.

Every hour or so he'd take a fifteen minute break, and during nine out of ten of those breaks he'd introduce a blues trio called the Rolling Stones. Up would jump Brian Jones, Keith Richards, and Mick Jagger to play with whichever of Korner's Blues Incorporated were left onstage, usually Charlie Watts or Graham Bond. They'd play three songs to an audience busy talking, buying drinks, yelling at each other, or whistling at the band because they were so damned young. Back then, you listened to the Stones, but you didn't take them seriously. Brian Jones played slide guitar, and their big tune was Elmore James's "Dust My Broom," which they'd stretch out to kill time. Jagger acted like he knew he was good; they all looked like they were proud, even though they hadn't slept for a couple of days. After each song, a few people sort of clapped, but most whistled and heckled the band. The thundering applause they saved for Alexis.

We must've seen the Stones ten times before Tim realized that Brian's guitar was tuned to a chord, so even if his left hand never touched the neck, the strings would sound great. That's how he could slide that glass tube up and down the guitar. Those guys were definitely smarter than they looked, we thought. After the last break, they'd walk across the street and ride the tube to God knows where.

When it was time for Cam and me to start thinking about what we were going to do after high school graduation, of course our thoughts turned to Ealing Art School, the college Tim attended. I had visited it once with Tim and marveled at his autonomy there, how he could go anywhere, say anything, work on stuff, not work on stuff. After a cup of tea, he took me to his life drawing class, which was a life-altering experience for me.

We walked into a huge room that smelled of turpentine and linseed oil and was illuminated by skylights. Twenty easels were scattered around a small wooden platform about the size of the stage at the Ealing Club. A gramophone in the back of the room played jazz, Charlie Mingus's "Better Get Hit in Your Soul." Soon a tall woman wandered in. She looked like a housewife in a bathrobe. She stood on the stage, some guy brought her a chair, and she calmly took off her robe and tossed it over the seat back. She sat down, totally naked, and looked right at me, the only guy in the room who didn't have a pen, pencil, or brush in his hand, the only guy with his mouth stuck in the open-but-still-breathing position. From that moment, I knew I wanted to attend Ealing. I wanted to get paint all over my jeans and listen to jazz while rain beat on the skylights. Not surprisingly, when my stepfather learned I wanted to go to what amounted to a free college, he was very supportive.

I wound up in the photography section of Ealing by mistake. I was terrified of the art induction test: you went into the studio, they gave you sketch paper and a piece of charcoal, said, "Okay, let's see what you can do," and hit the stopwatch. To gather strength and courage, I took a walk around the school and, in my wanderings, stumbled onto the photography department. I didn't know it, but at that time it was regarded as the best photography school in Europe. Unlike the rest of the college, there was no test to get in, just an interview with the headmaster, whose fascination with me was not the lies I fed him about my uncle the photographer and how I always wanted to learn and now I wanted to do this for a profession because. . . . Rather, he dug me because there were no Americans in his course. The headmaster had a big world map marked to show the homes of his students: Australia, New Zealand, Africa, China. Not one thumbtack on America. When I walked in, he couldn't wait to throw a tack on Florida.

To enroll at Ealing, you had to convince the faculty that you were out to be a great artist of some kind. You had to show heart. Talent helped, too, but I didn't have any talent that I knew of. Surprisingly, during my eighteen months at Ealing, I managed to win awards and keep work up on display alongside some truly amazing student art. The unorthodox theory of the school was not to hire schoolteachers, but rather professionals, and hope they could be teachers for two or three hours a week. For example, a guy would come in to teach our fashion photography class who'd been shooting in London seven days a week for British *Vogue*.

Ealing was exciting—for everyone. At the American high school, if you came in late, the teacher took down your name. At Ealing, no one ever took attendance, no bells ever rang. Students would be lined up behind the janitors when they opened the school early in the morning; it was the kind of place you couldn't wait to get into. Lots of times we stayed until ten at night.

There were several thousand students at the school, which was divided into the departments of fashion design, photography, fine arts, and graphic arts. The art departments were the top of the heap at Ealing, the cutting edge of the school. Students' work would be hung in the display areas, album and magazine covers from the graphic arts kids. From fine arts, you'd be walking to your classroom and you'd see a normal-looking painting on a canvas, only it would be hand-sawn halfway across, torn, tattered, and ripped.

The battle cry at Ealing was "Art is more than just a dusty bowl of fruit." The challenge was to do something mind-blowing, build a following, make changes for the better by making waves. At Ealing, there were always the "what ifs": what if you did a series of paintings that self-destructed at the exhibition? What if you made up a language; could you teach it to anyone else if that was the only language you spoke? The whole school was a pressure cooker of artistic energy. People weren't studying so they could go out and make money. The idea was to go out and do something worthwhile—like change the world.

Another tack went up on America when Cam enrolled at Ealing. His mom was moving the family back to the U.S., and he wanted to stay in England. I did, too. My family was returning to the States—Texas, to ease my mom's bronchitis. So I was to finish my studies at Ealing. With both Cam and I now needing a place to stay, Tim set out to find digs for the three of us, and in a week or two, came up with the flat on Sunnyside Road, two blocks from school. We rented the top floor, or rather, the room that was the top floor. The bathroom was down the stairs on a landing between the third and second floors. Rent was five pounds a week. Split three ways, this worked.

Things were cramped in the flat, but we erected a musical shrine of sorts as the focal point. Record player stacked on a cardboard box, albums lined up wall to wall on both sides like musical encyclopedias. When we combined my records with Tim's and Cam's, we had over 300 albums, which was a big deal in those days. Collectively, we had every record that Jimmy Reed, Chuck Berry, Ray Charles, Elvis, Buddy Holly, and Booker T. and the MGs had ever made, plus Mose Allison, John Lee Hooker, Muddy Waters, Jimmy Smith, Howlin' Wolf, Jerry Lee Lewis, and even three Jonathan Winters albums. Plus, we had stacks and stacks of 45s. We rarely played those, though, because you had to get up and change the record after every song.

One day between classes, Tim rushed up to me, gasping, "You've got to come to the commons room and see this guy play guitar!" I hurried over. There was Pete, seated in the corner, a big-nosed kid strumming Tim's beat-up acoustic. A small cluster of students surrounded him. His playing was spectacular. He was using bar chords, putting his finger on the fret and changing keys. No one I knew could do that. We were all amazed; we didn't want him to stop. He'd finish a song, and we'd urge him to play a little longer. He played for about ten minutes then finally put the guitar down.

I was stunned. I had to hear more. Maybe he could show us how to play like that, I thought.

I invited him to come over to the flat after classes. It felt more like coaxing. "I've got Chuck Berry records," I told him, "I've got Jimmy Reed." Pete had never heard of Jimmy Reed. He said he didn't even have a record player.

When he stood up, he was tall and looked like a character straight out of Dickens: jeans, tweed jacket, scarf, floppy hair. He had a group, he told me, a band that played at clubs around town. I'd never met anyone in a real band before.

Later, he'd say I was the first student at Ealing ever to speak to him.

CHAPTER SIX

Pot

And so Pete started coming over. I'd spin him records that he'd never heard. He'd sit there with a guitar and play. I had an electric, a Fender we'd plug into the phonograph. He'd play along with the records and make the music sound even better than it already was. Just as fast as we could change the LPs, he'd keep playing. It soon became our ritual: school, and then back to the flat to listen to music. Our world revolved around music and Ealing, plus Sid's Café, the coffee shop across from school where the art students hung out. One day we took the best of our 45s into the café. The jukebox there was filled with Elvis impersonators and Buddy Holly knockoffs, so we talked the owner into letting us put in our "Green Onions" and Jimmy Reed and Chuck Berry singles.

At the flat that first day, I turned Pete on to pot. I had only recently been introduced to it myself. Tim and Cam and I would go down to Soho to hear live music. The clubs there catered mostly to Jamaicans and black American GIs on weekends. They were mostly basement clubs, dark and smoky. By the time you made it downstairs, you'd be stoned because everybody in the room was smoking. Everyone, even the GIs, was well-dressed. It was a whole new world, very polite and elite in its own way. There was a rhythm to the whole thing. People seemed to be all on the same plane. I was fascinated by how civil it all was. It was a warm feeling, the polar opposite of what we'd always been told about marijuana. There was no chaos or violence or insanity, so discovering pot, I thought that I'd unlocked the secret to the universe. And I wanted to share it with everybody who was close to me.

By the time Pete walked into Sunnyside, we'd been smoking pot for a year. It was a part of our routine, a fun, smart secret that we shared, though it was literally sweeping London at the time. We tried to recreate the Soho club atmosphere in our flat. We'd come back from school and smoke pot and drink English beer from big liter-size bottles and put on a Jimmy Reed album and just let it play. At night, we'd close the curtains and switch on a red safelight bulb, and then light a candle so we wouldn't waste matches firing up our endless joints and pipes.

When Pete came over that first day, it was a bit delicate. We were shy about introducing something that we'd always been taught was a no-no. But

Ron Wood
last Faces tour, 1975

we started playing records, and soon I just rolled a joint like it was a normal thing to do. Pete joined the ritual from day one. As soon as he started feeling the high that first time, his reaction was, "This is great. This is really great." He took to it immediately, the elevation of awareness, like you'd just gone through a door, like you understood more of what was going on. It was like having the key to the combination lock that led you into what seemed like the real world. You were in a sensible awareness—and it felt good. Then we learned we could smoke a joint before we went to school and it would be more fun still. Then we'd come home and smoke, and it was back and forth and back and forth.

Joe Walsh and James Gang roadie Mark Patterson
Kent Hotel, Ohio, 1969

Suddenly, Pete went from being very reserved and shy, not saying much to anyone, to an incredible fountain of articulate thought and conversation. His words painted pictures; I knew he was an artist without ever having seen a sketch. There was strength to his words. He could talk and explain something in a way that made it seem solid. He spoke the way he played guitar. This wasn't someone who just played scales. Pete played the right note at the right time, notes that not only went along with whatever was playing on the record player, but that made the record stronger and better. Meaningful. Records that I'd been listening to for years took on new layers of significance, thanks to Pete.

After a while, as Pete relaxed and realized that he was welcome at the flat, that we enjoyed his company, he began to reveal himself. We discovered he had the ability to use different accents and different personas, that he had a wicked sense of humor, that he could make sense of any situation, and also make a joke about it. It was like unwrapping a package and finding this unparalleled energy beneath the paper.

I learned that as a teen, when most kids were out raising hell, Pete spent a lot of time at home alone playing guitar. It was where he felt most comfortable. His father was a union musician, part of a popular big band ensemble since before the war. On occasion, when his father's group played a local gig, his whole family would come along and peek out from behind the curtain at the lights and audience.

I learned that Pete entered Ealing in 1960 because it was close, free, and fairly obscure. He could fade into the landscape of London's scruffy art students, keep his head down, and apply himself to his graphic arts course. It was simple economics that led him to form his first band, the Detours. Hitting the stage to bring home some bacon was simply the way of life for the Townshends.

I saw the Detours once with Cam in January 1963, at the Fox & Goose Hotel in Ealing, a large pub with a stage within walking distance of the school. Pete didn't play an electric guitar that night, just an acoustic with a pickup under the strings, plus a banjo. The Detours had a singer, a bass player who'd play a little trumpet sometimes, and a drummer who looked like somebody's dad or older brother and didn't seem to be having much fun. Pete's friend Roger Daltrey played harmonica and maracas and sang a bit. Pete didn't sing, but he'd yell and tell jokes. They did "I Walk the Line," the Johnny Cash song; an Elvis tune; some Carl Perkins; and highlighted the gig with Pete's rendering of a Chet Atkins guitar solo.

It was amazing to me that the Detours didn't have stage fright. I always liked to keep a low profile; seeing people onstage intentionally drawing attention to themselves was a whole new concept for me. I mostly watched Pete, though. He moved around a lot, cavorting onstage as though it was what you were supposed to do, like it was normal human behavior. Cam and I didn't enjoy the show much. We were happy to see Pete play, but he didn't sound nearly as good as he did in the flat.

The Detours played the NCO clubs at American air bases in England, mostly to GIs, with an occasional English date. Pete approached work with the band with the same determination he would've had growing up in Detroit working the assembly line at the Ford plant. Music was the natural way to earn money. That one-on-one communication that had heretofore been awkward and difficult for him was possible with an audience, and he pushed his newfound outlet to the limits of the audience's nerves. Standard procedure was to gulp a half-pint of brandy before going on; with the invisible protective buzz, his humor, and his explosive energy—often out-and-out aggression—he kept his audiences on the brink and curious.

Music was a lifeline for him, and, aided in no small part by his time at Sunnyside, he soon became an expert on American R&B and country rock. But it went beyond the notes. I felt the same way. My record collection was about more than the music. I bought one of the John Lee Hooker EPs simply because of its cover. Here's a guy standing out on a dirt road, his hat sort of turned off to the side, playing an electric guitar, oblivious to anything commercial. He wasn't posing for that photograph. It was real. And on that record was "Crawling King Snake," "Boogie Chillen"—greasy, gutsy, potent stuff. The impact of that record, though, was not so much in the notes that Hooker played, but the attitude with which he played them. Your first reaction was, my God, the guitar is out of tune, but the guy's still playing like it doesn't really matter. And most of my records were like that. Booker T. was not trying to be Bobby Rydell. The music had an underground feel to it. The artists weren't trying to trick you into listening. It was real. Genuine. Listening to this stuff, you lost touch with the society in which you grew up and found yourself digging into this new society, with its entirely different set of values. Pete got it immediately and took it to another level, not just musically, but philosophically, as well. Doors were opening for him, I could tell.

At Sunnyside we had camaraderie, fellowship, and more music than any kid in England had ever seen. We'd get so stoned, you couldn't move. If you could roll over to the stack of records, all you had to do was simply choose one, and with a glance at the song list find a cut that would fry anyone in the room. If, by some horrible misfortune, you got a bad cut, some song that was just awful, the mood shattered like a glass. Everyone had the same reaction. A record that was bullshit was a manifestation of some ugly universal truth. A wasted track was like a wasted life; filling in the blanks was a crime. Being that stoned, a record that was trying to pull the wool over your eyes produced instant, excruciating pain. But those moments were kept to a minimum at Sunnyside. There, creating the perfect atmosphere was everyone's full-time job.

Not everybody liked the scene at Sunnyside. Roger would show up occasionally when it was time for a Detours gig. He was the driver; he'd blow the horn outside. If we were listening to records or rolling another joint, we'd simply postpone answering the door. Roger didn't like that; by the time he got into the flat he was disenchanted, to say the least, with the low lights, the music, and the fact that the band was late for the gig. For Roger, it was a distraction from good business practice.

Soon a flat beneath ours opened up and Pete moved in. It was the perfect setup. He had access to a treasure trove of records, we had the pleasure of the company of a witty, wily guitar player who made things better just by showing up. He was always out of the building by the time Cam and I rose in the morning, even if we were up early. His logic: if he went to class, did his assignments, worked on his projects first thing, the rest of the afternoon was his to smoke dope and soak up American blues. Same for gig nights. He had his own ritual: the bath, the wardrobe, the cologne, the joints. He'd get himself ready hours before Roger was to come over to fetch him. That way, he could come upstairs to our flat and get more stoned before the show. When Roger blew the horn and Pete tore himself away, the flat seemed empty. There was nothing left to do but go to the pub.

Pete Townshend
1968

One morning, as Cam and I were walking through the school's glass and
chrome lobby on the way to class, we crossed paths with a good-looking
blond guy carrying a cloth suitcase. We mumbled, "Good morning," and he
came back with an eager, "Hi!" I stopped in my tracks. English guys didn't
say "hi."

"Are you American?" I asked. As the only Americans out of 6,000 at Ealing,
Cam and I had a good thing going—lonely female students loved Americans,
or at least we believed they did. We were practically celebrities. The last
thing we needed was a handsome competitor.

"California," he said, and thrust out his hand. "Do you guys go to school here?"

We needed to know this guy's story, so we offered to buy him coffee at Sid's. Over steaming mugs he introduced himself as Franklin Sturgis, but we could call him Frank. He was hitchhiking through Europe before he started school at UCLA, he told us. Sounded important; we were impressed. He'd been all over, he said, Spain, Scandinavia, had even worked in a TV assembly plant in Holland. Said he was hitching his way to Southampton to stay with his sister, who'd married an English guy. He planned to take a passenger ship to New York, then eventually fly back to California. Wow, we thought, this guy's fearless, and interesting. We invited him to stay for a day or two at the flat and he accepted. We pointed him in the direction of the coin laundry, Ealing Library, and the nearest pub, and made plans to meet back in the lobby that afternoon. Neither Cam nor I wanted to miss our fashion photography class—our teacher always brought a beautiful model or two.

Frank stayed at Sunnyside a couple of days, ironed all his clothes, took a bath. He was pleasant and interesting and we loved having him around. On his last day, we finally talked him into smoking some pot. Frank was a drinker, didn't even smoke cigarettes, and the idea of smoking some kind of weed just bored him. But when he realized we weren't just smoking, we were getting high, he decided to give it a try.

He loved it, stayed another day, and then announced he'd be on his way in the morning. We joked around some, and as he was folding up the ironing board, Frank's passport fell out of his shirt pocket onto the floor. I picked it up and thumbed through it. It was a habit of mine—the more stamps in your passport, the more worldly you seemed to me. It was a status thing. I glanced at the picture. It was of a guy with a beard. He wasn't handsome . . . and he wasn't blond.

"Hey, that's not you," I said. We both stopped laughing.

Frank grabbed the passport and shoved it in his back pocket. "I look different with a beard," he muttered.

It definitely wasn't him, but he sure as hell didn't want to talk about it. I let it drop.

Next morning, he thanked us for everything and we all headed out, Frank for the tube station, Cam and I for school. The passport incident was still heavy on my mind. Cam, who hadn't seen the guy's picture, assured me it didn't mean anything, that we'd both soon forget the whole episode. He was right. We went right back to our school/pot/getting-Pete-to-play-guitar-with-the-records routine, Pete nailing Chuck Berry, Bo Diddley, and Elmore James with no problem.

Two weeks later, Cam, Tim, Tim's girlfriend, and I stayed late at school one night to catch the film *Jazz on a Summer's Day*. Someone had told us Chuck Berry was in it, so we were eager to see it. Unfortunately, the projector broke. Disappointed, Cam and I headed back to Sunnyside, and Tim took his girlfriend back to her parents' house.

Paris, 1964

The next morning I hopped the bus to the Ealing tube station, and then took the tube to the train station. I boarded a train for Paris, carrying only a shoulder bag and a camera. Everything else I'd left for Pete: my records, my Levi's, my electric guitar.

Alone and moving, I felt good. I didn't want a car, didn't even want a bicycle. It was easy to find a cheap place to stay. And it was a thrill to live on whatever I could earn with a camera. For an eighteen-year-old American alone in the City of Lights, things just happened. I started photographing artists, first the ones on the sidewalk, the guys with the easels and pastels. They never took me seriously—just another guy with a camera that they'd never see again. But when I came back the next day with prints, they went crazy. I started making money right away. Artists always needed pictures. Word spread. Eventually, I was invited to shoot artists with studio ateliers, attics with skylights, like in the movies, like the art studios at Ealing, peopled with Scandinavian and American coeds posing as exotic street urchins, girls drinking wine and modeling for money. Then came the writers, the café writers, and, occasionally, a wandering musician. I met an American guitar player who made a hundred dollars a day just playing for people queued up at the cinema and then blew it all on heroin for himself and his Swedish girlfriend who passed the hat.

The year I spent in Paris was the most time I spent around other photographers. There were loads of them from all over the world, none as young as me. These were guys trying to make it big, get discovered, pull assignments for *Vogue* or *Time*. They were the starving photographers, staying busy mostly in cafés.

Dicken & kitten
Ibiza, 1964

In Paris, people leave the cafés only to go to work or sleep. You go to a museum and spend a few hours at an art show, and then talk about it for weeks in the café. Every crowd has its café: the fags ("fags" was the polite term; Americans preferred "queers"), the jazz guys, students, terrorists, whores, models, whatever.

Even the starving art photographers had a café, Le Tournon, in the Ninth Arrondissement, the Polish/Algerian ghetto. You wandered in and it was nothing but empty tables and photographers. Kind of a remake of the common room at Ealing. Le Tournon was never too busy, and nobody minded if you used the empty tables to spread out portfolio shots. The old-timers who had their own apartments, their own darkrooms, and could speak French, they were the most interesting. Most of us sat on the edge of our chairs and listened to them talk.

Once a month they would hit you up for 100 francs, twenty bucks. They put all the money in a stack then drew a name from a hat. If it was yours, you had enough to go to a hot spot. In those days, it was Algeria and Cyprus war zones. Those pictures were guaranteed sales, big money. It took nine months for my name to come up, and when it did I suddenly had $220, more money than I'd ever felt in my pockets at one time. I hopped a train to Barcelona, Spain, for $15, and then an overnight passenger steamboat to the island of Ibiza, 500 miles out in the Mediterranean. I checked into a peasant hotel for thirty-five cents a day. I felt like Howard Hughes without the Kleenex. I stayed eighteen months.

Pete and I kept in touch while I was in Europe. I'd write him about the solo guitar players making money off the foreigners. Once he sent me a letter about hearing the first Donovan record and how good he thought it was. Bob Dylan had met his match, he wrote. While I was in Ibiza I received a postcard saying he'd changed the name of his band to the High Numbers, and later, a letter telling me that he'd written a song called "My Generation" that he thought I might dig.

When I moved from Ibiza to Formentera, the smallest island in the Balearic chain, I found that I didn't even miss having electricity. Formentera was paradise. I lived by candlelight in a stone peasant's house with a good well. Wine was thirty-five cents a liter, cigarettes seven cents a pack. Every day the boat would cross over from Ibiza. There were always new French and Scandinavian girls coming to the island for a day or two to round out their vacation. Formentera was only six miles long, so you didn't need a car. And a shortwave radio was all you needed for entertainment. You could read a paperback novel a day. Get a suntan. Go to the only bar on the island, get loaded, and have sex with a complete stranger who would get up the next day and take the boat back to wherever they'd come from.

Dicken and Florence
Ibiza, 1964

I turned twenty-one on Formentera. An American couple threw a party for me in their house. About ten people were there. Someone had made party hats out of newspaper, and there was wine punch, gallons of vino in a huge pot with a ladle, with some orange slices floating on top. What gave the party real pow was the twenty or so hits of pure Benzedrine dumped in with each new batch. The fiesta went on for six days. The sun went up and

Paris, 1963

down like a big yellow yo-yo while we all talked and laughed and talked some more. I'd like to say I never forgot it. Fact is, after I finally went home and crashed for a couple of days, all I could remember was blowing out a bunch of candles, paper hats, and the sun through the windows going up and down. Up and down.

After a year I got on the boat and headed back to where I'd come from. It was either that or stay there forever. I thought I was wise and that the time had come to apply my wisdom to fulfilling some kind of future. I really believed that I'd figured everything out. Life. Women. Retirement. Art. Money. Music. Family. I knew how it all worked, and I could either stay here in paradise or go back to the States like a man, face the draft notice I'd been carrying around in my back pocket for nine months, and build an adult life.

By the time I got off the plane in the middle of the night in my family's latest hometown of San Antonio, Texas, I'd forgotten everything. I gawked at the squeaky-scrubbed people in starched clothing with expressions that said, "I know where I'm going, that's why I'm walking swiftly, standing tall, and appearing successful," only to find that they were marching to the snack bar or the restroom. Suddenly, it was painfully obvious that I'd landed in the world of robots—and it was just a matter of time before I'd be found out.

Soon it was back to Florida. My family moved to some property that had actually belonged to my stepfather's dad, 200 uninhabited acres with a lake. We built a small house on an island in the lake. I begged for a job down the road as an underwater photographer at a dancing-mermaids tourist attraction, Weeki Wachee Springs, and began living from paycheck to paycheck.

Thank God for Pete's call. The Hermits tour saved me from giving up on all of the rebellious, arty thoughts that had spewed out of Ealing like a spiritual volcano, concepts reinforced in Paris and Ibiza as simple truths and common sense. Conversations that went on for days in Europe would end in the States in less than a minute with "So what?" Nobody cared about art here. Picasso was interesting only because he was rich. Artists were kooks, and now that the war was on, they were probably cowards too. In the U.S., a photographer sounded sort of legit and not as bad as an artist. Musicians weren't artists, they were misfits—almost the same, just as bad.

And musicians destroying their instruments? Well, it was outrageous, wasteful. Electric guitars were so expensive, especially American guitars.

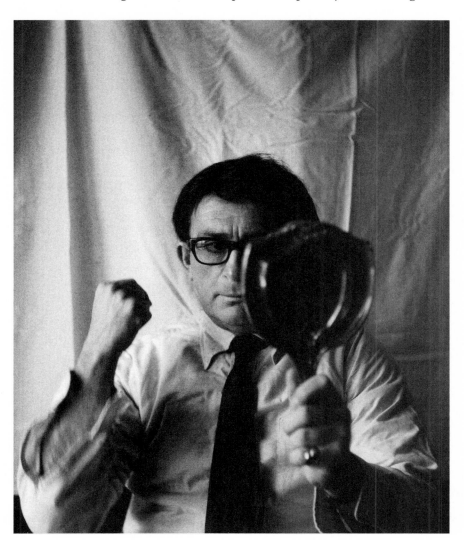

Elmer de Horay
infamous art forger adjusting his wig
for passport photo, Ibiza, 1963

Ibiza, 1963

Fenders—top of the line. I'd heard that when music stores in England learned Pete was busting up guitars, they wouldn't even sell them to him anymore. Destroying a perfectly useful instrument was sacrilege, plain and simple. To me, it was a brilliant expression of frustration; it took guts.

And actually, it was far from wasteful. Pete was always repairing his smashed guitars. There were really only two pieces to a Fender guitar: the main body, which was a big block of alder, and the neck, which was maple with a maple or rosewood fretboard so you wouldn't get splinters in your fingers. A steel rod ran up the middle of the neck for strength, so if you swung the guitar like a baseball bat at, say, a telephone pole, the neck would break free from the body. If you grasped the guitar by the neck like a butter churn and slammed the base down on a hard floor, it would eventually split like a piece of firewood. All the rest were pieces: the pickups, knobs, strings. Pete learned early on that if you split a solid piece of alder you'd wind up with two pieces that could be joined back together perfectly, not a zillion shards like if you shattered a china plate.

He used an English wood glue that came in a can, a fine white powder he'd mix with water, and he'd paint it onto the two broken edges. He'd join the pieces together with some gaffer's tape, like a zipper over the crack, and then wrap the whole thing in loops of rubber he'd cut from bicycle

Weeki Wachee Springs
1967

Pete Townshend
and Kit Lambert
Nashville, 1967

inner tubes. The next day, he'd find the body of the guitar stronger than before it was broken. In most cases, the neck had just fallen off, but if the neck was indeed broken, Pete simply replaced it. Since all Fender necks were interchangeable, Pete had boxes of necks, new and repaired, as well as boxes of bodies, extra pickups, and knobs and switches. Each guitar would be smashed multiple times, and when it became clear that the guitars never, ever broke where they'd been glued, the glue manufacturer used that fact as a product endorsement.

If we had an extra day or even a half-day on the Hermits tour, Christopher "Kit" Lambert, half the Who's management team—Chris Stamp was his partner—and all of the band's sound production team at the time would catch a flight from England and look for a studio near where we were staying. We'd go to any studio Kit could find in the yellow pages that had multitrack two-inch machines, state of the art at the time. Multitrack meant that you could record a song using just two tracks, say, and then you could add whatever you wanted to the others. For the Who, this meant Kit could record the band live in England using two tracks, and then later, take the tapes into any multitrack studio and add other instruments or more vocals, or play tapes recorded earlier and add stuff, subtract stuff, experiment.

Studios with multitrack recorders went for $100 an hour, engineer extra. Kit would locate a new studio, go check out the facility's equipment, make sure the engineer was cool and that the doors would lock, and then he would send for the band. He'd give me a call and I'd round up whomever

he needed and drive them over to the studio. Kit would have a tape—about the circumference of a small garbage can lid, two inches thick, about twenty pounds—cued and ready, and when he was finished, he'd tip the engineer, take the tape, and that would be that.

Eventually, the tape would be finished, all the tracks filled the way Kit wanted them, and he'd go into a studio and mix. To mix, he'd have two tape machines. The original tape would go through a mixing board that had controls for each track, which he would adjust, and the result would be captured on a second tape. If on one track Keith was singing out of tune or it simply sounded bad, Kit could pull the volume down to nothing and Keith wouldn't even appear on the new mixdown tape.

Kit would stick on a Who multitrack demo and blast it on the studio playback speakers at absolute full volume. This served not only to check the speakers, but as a warning to the studio engineer that things were going to be loud and dangerous. When the guitar kicked in, it sounded like a jet fighter taking off in your face. Entwistle has said that the drum sound Kit got out of Keith on record made him sound like he was "banging on biscuit tins." In the studio, it sounded like World War III.

Pete Townshend and Russ Gibb at WKNR radio Detroit, playing the only copy of Tommy in town, 1969

CHAPTER EIGHT

Old Secrets

The meeting with Pete was like sticking my fingers into the wall socket and transferring thirty years of gaps into one cohesive loop, something that older folks can do. In that room, with our cups of English tea, seated at the long table and gazing out at the river, all the boring and painful parts had fallen away and only, thank God, the profound stuff that was worth talking about was left. The profound stuff . . . that's what they'd taught us to look for at Ealing.

Kids okay? Yeah. Girlfriend okay? Yeah. Money, heart, health? Yeah, yeah, yeah. Now what about the book? Pete had been pushing me for years to write it.

"You are a secret," Pete told me, "and now you are an old secret. We are both old secrets. Some of the press over here thinks I'm . . . you don't even want to know. You get sidetracked and think, well, at least someone in my organization is watching out for bullshit. But, no, new bullshit arrives every day, and I have to shovel it off the walkway myself or it builds up until we all grind to a halt."

He shifted gears. "You've got to come back over here after the tour. We could do a documentary about you and those fucking records, maybe a radio show. You never got your records back, did you?" he asked.

"Back? I thought you had them in your basement for forty years," I said.

"No, no," said Pete. "Barney and I shipped them off to Spain or Paris, I don't remember which. But I do remember I ordered and bought and replaced every one of those records. It cost £30,000. Some records were so rare it cost hundreds of pounds just for one LP."

Later, Pete would tell me that Barney, his old roommate, felt he deserved half the replacement albums Pete bought since Barney had, after all, paid the rent at least once. But Pete wasn't up for that. To make amends, Pete said that many years later he'd taken Barney record shopping and let him buy as much music as he liked. On those shopping trips, Pete and Barney together would rack up as much as $30,000.

Roger Daltrey
second photo session
with the Who, Ohio

Richard Barnes was on tour a lot of times when I wasn't. Barney was in Cincinnati when those eleven kids got trampled to death in '79, and he was also there in the earliest of days, when the band was making the transition from Sunnyside Road to full-time roadwork.

When the guys were going crazy to find a cool name, it was a blasted Barney, standing under the red lights with a liter of beer in his hand, who suggested "the Who." "The Who, what a great name. . . . "

Barney's still pretty much intact, Pete told me, though he hasn't seen him in years. And whereas Pete smoked and drank to excess and fell from grace, Barney smoked and drank in a very proper, very English pub way. After any given day, when the heavy lifting was done, Barney's big line had always been, "Fancy a drink?" Meaning he was off to the pub to drink beer, play darts, listen to music, and find someone to fall for. It was so English, made so much sense. But after Pete forced himself to quit smoking, managed to stop drinking, and after several hospital interventions finally stopped taking drugs, he couldn't be around people who smoked or drank. Especially Barney. Barney would stop making sense around dark, and that was the time Pete was usually ready to work on stuff.

Pete Townshend
and Tom Wright
outside Eel Pie, 2006

Pete exhaled through his lips and laughed. "I still love Barney, but life is just a lot simpler if he doesn't come around."

I'd seen Barney at the convention the day before. He'd walked in carrying a box of books and did a double take when he saw me. "I thought you were dead," he said. "I was in Thailand on holiday and heard you had died of a heart attack. But obviously, you didn't." I followed him out to his car as he pulled out another box of books, the two titles Barney wrote years ago, *The Who: Maximum R&B* and *Mods!*, both of which still sell. Proud of himself for delivering the merchandise, Barney closed the trunk and rolled down his sleeves. "Look at us," he said. "Sixty years old. Who would have guessed we'd have made it this far? Fancy a drink?"

A soft knock at the door brought me back to the moment. It was Brian, the kid, letting Pete know his car was on the way. We stood up, hands still on the tops of the teacups.

"You should stick around," Pete said. "I'll only be gone an hour or so, and we plan to work in the studio this afternoon. Rachel and I were going to France today, but now we're leaving in the morning." We returned the cups to the kitchen; Pete rinsed them out then grabbed his coat. I picked up my bag and followed him down through the lobby.

Before we stepped outside, Pete stopped. "It's time for you to get things in order," he told me. "So many people are telling so many stories that are about fuck-all, and here you are with a story that is worth telling—and you're not telling it." He was right.

We were standing in a circle outside Eel Pie; Pete and I, Rogan, and Pridden. Pete started telling his Elton John story. I'd heard it before, but it'd been years. I was sure Rogan had heard it, and Pridden had probably heard it every single time Pete had told it. But it was still funny. In the mid-'90s, Pete and Elton John were on the same Concorde flight to New York, so they sat together. Halfway across the Atlantic, all the engines on the right side blew out. The plane bounced and shook, people were moaning and wailing, and Pete was thinking he was gonna die, he told us, which would've been very inconvenient. But before he could get totally freaked, Elton John started to cry, sobbed "like a baby girl," Pete said, "and he would not shut up." It was as loud and desperate as a movie soundtrack, he told us. Then some lunatic, dressed like a rabbi with the robe and beard and clutching a black metal box, tried to force open the cockpit door in front of them. "This has to get to New York, no matter what!" the rabbi screamed over and over. Elton, transfixed by the guy, ceased his whimpering, while Pete was certain they were either gonna crash or the rabbi was gonna set off a bomb. Ultimately, they made an emergency landing in Greenland.

We were all still chuckling as Pete's car pulled up. On impulse, I handed Rogan the digital camera he'd given me and asked him to take a shot.

One snap and Pete was off.

Holiday Inn, America's First One-Hour Photo Lab

On tour in the '60s and '70s, I fixed up the hotel bathrooms with five or six red bulbs, which gave them that whorehouse look. There seemed to be something illicit about the place. The bands would go down the freight elevators thinking, "Well, we'll just sneak into Tom's room." The choice was standing around in an empty room drinking Dr. Pepper and eating bologna and cheese crackers, or joining me in the darkroom and seeing 11x14s of yourself from onstage a half-hour earlier. No contest.

Joe Walsh wouldn't let me do it alone. He always wanted to be the darkroom assistant. He'd play guitar while I mixed up the chemicals, but when I started printing, I'd hand him the paper and he'd do the developing. Rod Stewart just liked to look at the images. Townshend wanted to get involved, fiddle around with equipment, screw with the enlarger, blow things up.

It was fun for everybody. How could it not be fun? The picture was only forty-five minutes old. Someone would ask, "Well, did you get a shot of Pete busting up his guitar?" Well, sure. Well, let's see it. Let's blow it up six feet high. Let's glue it on the door.

Hotel darkroom
Faces tour, mid-'70s

Instant visual feedback. The guys were used to having their pictures made, seeing a contact sheet a week or two later, and then getting the prints a week or two after that. Maybe an album cover or two a year. I didn't have that kind of time. I'd look at the negatives and print up the good ones right then and there, thirty or forty after each show. One-hour photo lab—right in the hotel bathtub.

Pete'd look at the photos, study them, make fun of the funny ones. It was a way for the band to see what they normally couldn't. They weren't being filmed, so there was no playback of the show. The photos were immediate documentation of the night, like taking notes. If the pictures looked good, it made the band want to look even better. If Roger's fur coat was too fuzzy and awkward, he'd look at the photo and you'd never see the coat again. It was the Ealing thing, creative energy going around and around.

We'd check into the hotel about three or four in the afternoon and call room service to say we needed more towels. They'd send up the 200-pound maid who'd give us four and say that was all she had.

Before she left, I'd say, "Hold it right there, just hold those towels. I'm testing out this roll of film." And I'd try to take a shot that made her look like a fashion model, sizzling hot. Then I'd process it, call the front desk asking for her again, and learn that she'd be in at eight in the morning. When she comes in and finds an 11x14 of *Marilou with Towels*, she goes wild and brings towels by the truckload.

Model for a day

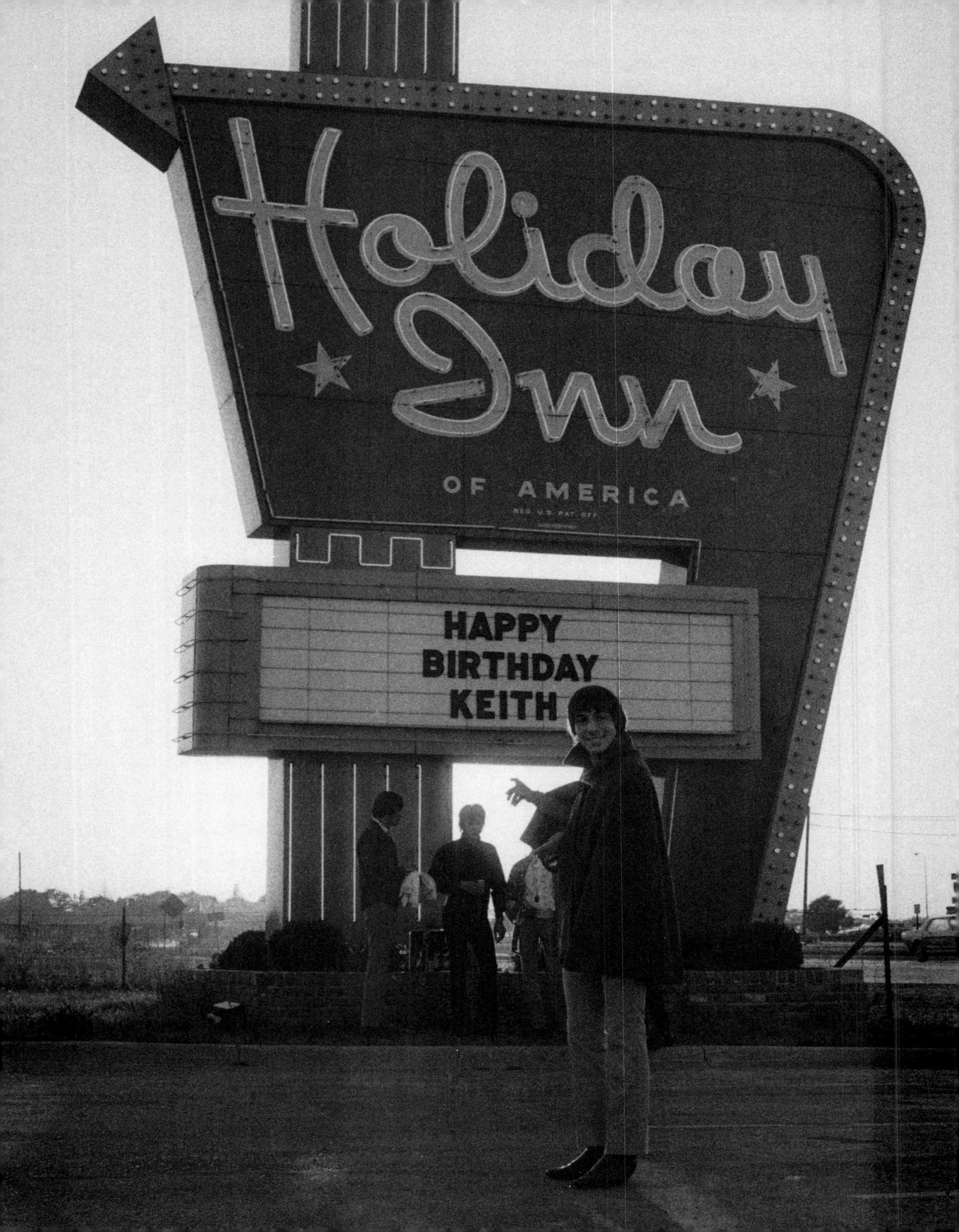
Holiday Inn
OF AMERICA
HAPPY
BIRTHDAY
KEITH

Keith's Birthday

Living at the Holiday Inn was like trying to have a frat party at your grandmother's. We were all carrying portable record players—this was before personal headphones—and as soon as the volume hit a certain level, the other hotel guests, whom we regarded as grown-ups, would have the hallways crawling with cops, making us apologize and turn down the volume and otherwise act humble until everyone calmed down. The whole idea of people under thirty traveling in large numbers and invading motels was sort of like the pot-smokers' freedom march.

Keith Moon's twenty-first birthday at the Holiday Inn in Flint, Michigan, in '67—well, that was like a longhair revolution.

Keith was the youngest member of the band, which explained his terminal cuteness and never-ending supply of boyish pranks. When the Who toured Europe and England, Keith could walk into any bar and order up whatever booze he wanted. In America, however, bartenders demanded ID. And so I became, among other things, the enabler, the guy in the bar who slid Moon his drinks.

As his twentieth birthday neared, Keith decided that what he really needed was a stack of newspaper headlines screaming, "Keith Turns 21!" that he could flash to dubious bartenders, settling once and for all his legalness. A plan was hatched.

We'd be in Flint on his birthday, August 23, so a party was thrown together at the Holiday Inn there. Music industry VIPs were invited, as well as every press person within a hundred miles. I was instructed to get a shot of Keith in front of the hotel marquee, develop it, and distribute 8x10s to the media. Much to Keith's dismay, instead of saying, "Happy 21st Keith," the marquee simply read, "Happy Birthday Keith."

Keith Moon
Flint, Michigan, 1967

Soon the party was in full swing in the hotel conference room, which was festooned with crepe paper streamers and a "21" banner the record label people had brought from New York. Folding banquet tables draped with white tablecloths held stacks of paper plates, plastic spoons, a dozen identical five-tiered chocolate cakes, and two huge punch bowls, one filled with pink lemonade, the other, scotch and coke, up until that day the only thing Keith would drink. No doubt the scotch was probably the best they could find, but that bowl just kind of sat there, occasionally catching a wandering deejay by surprise. The booze shortage meant that anyone who wanted something other than Keith's god-awful scotch and coke had to push open the double conference room doors to get to the bar, place a drink order, and return once more through the doors to await the cocktail's delivery.

Chris Stamp
at Premier Talent office
New York, 1967

CHAPTER ELEVEN

The Magoos

The tour was the center of the world. My world, at least.

My first real job, the gig shooting postcards of the mermaids at Weeki Wachee Springs in Florida, had been so unorthodox that it'd felt okay. Okay, but small. I could've died underwater messing with those air hoses and it would've been a little thing. A big day with charter buses bringing in crowd after crowd was still just a little thing.

That first Who tour? Now that was a constant Big Thing. For everyone. If Moon got into a bar fight, which he often did, the Who would all rush in to save him. Actually, if anyone got too close to any edge, anybody on the tour, pilot included, would throw themselves into the problem. Everything was a big deal, and the biggest thing of all was the tour itself. The plane would fly no matter what, and you couldn't miss anything, much less the flight.

The pace was full-throttle. The packing and unpacking. Hotel hallways filled to the brim with the prettiest, usually buzzed and purring, girls you ever saw, a few even over the age of sixteen. The dash to the plane. Next airport. Running late. Can't miss soundcheck, screw the hotel, go straight to the gig. I kept my footlockers full of photo gear in constant motion, but they were nothing compared to the mountains of amps, guitars, and speakers in hard cases and on wheels that went with us everywhere. We were the A-Team charging into endless oncoming trains. Get to the crossroads. Get lost in a traffic jam.

Loft window
West Village
New York City, 1967

The Hermits tour ended in Honolulu. I'd shot reams of film every step of the way, processed and printed in Holiday Inn darkrooms. I'd run errands, looked after "the lads," even given them haircuts, mini-trims during photo shoots under Roger's tutelage. It was a hell of a ride and had me convinced that what I was able to do with a camera actually mattered. I'd taken shots where everyone at least looked okay, if not cool. Eventually, none of the band was afraid of me and my pictures. They trusted me. They realized we all had the same mission: make the band look great.

I went home to Florida to process and print up portfolio books, compilation albums for each band member to take home, give to their parents or girlfriends. It wasn't long before Chris Stamp sent for me and I wound up back with the band, who were holed up at the Gorham Hotel in New York City. They played a show on Long Island with the Blues Magoos opening for them, and then one in the Poconos Mountains. Pete and the band wanted me to travel on with them to England; the British government had other ideas. Despite the best efforts of the band's lawyers to persuade the authorities to forgive and forget, pot was a long way from mainstream in those days. I was still quite the dastardly criminal on that side of the world.

So it was finally over. Maybe I'd see Pete again—there was some talk of another U.S. tour in early 1968—but this adventure was complete.

Not long after, a letter arrived, written on TWA's in-flight stationery, obviously written before my summons to New York:

Dear Tom,

Much as a drag it was to say goodbye yesterday it was great to spend some time with you. It seems it's destined to be like that. I hope the last session is proving to hold some good stuff. Considering the obstructions and problems you had to work against, I still think you've taken the best photographs we've ever had done.

Apart from doing all the group's laundry, cutting their hair, and wiping their asses, you hit it off well with everyone anyway. I was pretty nervous at meeting you again in Florida and I expected you to present me with a bill for all the clothes you lost in our last encounter. The T-shirts I gave you don't half repay those amazing Levi's I snitched; and the hospitality I received in Sunnyside wasn't half repaid by the few hotel room excursions we took . . .

I'll do my best to get you into G.B. but I feel that if our solicitors are on it you'll probably get in without my help anyway. Let's hope. If not, I'll be pissed off and I'll see you in February '68. What can I say? Let's keep in touch, keep up the good gardening. Love to your family . . . Pete

Blues Magoos

So I stayed in the Blues Magoos band house in the Bronx and waited for the Who to send for me. In the meantime, I shot an album cover for the third Magoos album, *Basic Blues Magoos*, and hung out in the Mercury Records studios in Manhattan while the band recorded it. And I began to learn about New York, the most foreign country I'd ever been in. The drummer of the Blues Magoos, Geoff Daking, was the only Magoo who hadn't come from the Jewish ghetto. He lived in Connecticut and was the privileged son of an investment banker. He'd drive into the city for recording sessions, and then, because everyone got stoned and drank too much, wind up staying in town at cheap hotels.

Soon Geoff and I moved into a loft down on Houston Street, about five blocks south of the Village, top floor of a six-level factory building. It was huge, L-shaped, a wide-open space with two bathrooms. The ladies' room had a bathtub, the men's a shower. Rent was $600 a month.

There were three ways to get into the Houston Street loft. During business hours, there was a freight elevator operated by a black junkie fresh out of 'Nam. He was friendly and funny in the mornings; at lunchtime he'd shoot up and slump over in the corner, and then we'd run the elevator ourselves. The rest of the building was pretty much of a mystery. The basement was some kind of Mafia social club, there was a typewriter repair place on the third floor, and we heard there was somebody right under us but we never saw the same people twice.

After 5 PM, the stairs in back were the only way in, and if you brought home some chick from the Village, by the time she walked all the way up the six flights of cement steps she was all but worn out. Never mind that in those days we seemed to have an endless supply of speed, hash, painkillers, and Librium, a monster pill that was the downer of choice before Valium. To entice some young thing to walk through the combat zone and up the stairs for the drugs, chances were she was drunk, and by the sixth floor, chances were that she was sick. The third way to get to the loft was the fire escape, one of those old metal things that zigzagged over the outside of the building. It looked like it hadn't been touched in fifty years.

Geoff and I fixed up the loft, painted all the brick walls flat white, and scrubbed the floor until the wood looked fairly good. I had all the Who equipment that was too heavy or too broken to ship back to England; all those smashed guitars hung on stark white walls were breathtaking. Geoff had a set of drums set up at one end of the space, and I had a functional Stratocaster plugged into an outrageous Marshall stack.

Geoff really came through when he ordered us a phone booth—not an ordinary phone booth, but one built for Chinatown, brand-new. A red pagoda, complete with doors, and when you walked inside, the lights came on and it was a real honest-to-God phone booth. In the six months that we had it, no one ever came to take out the money. Geoff eventually learned how to get the dough out and jam the machine so that we'd always have a line. We'd accept long distance calls from anywhere, talk for hours, and never pay a dime. Then we swapped out the white lights in the booth for red. We'd go in there, shut the doors, the red lights and the fan would come on, and with a very little hash two or three people could get stoned for the price of one.

One night Geoff had just returned from a tour of Canada and wanted us to go down to the Village, get some steaks, get fucked up, and maybe get laid. We got the steaks, but no snatch, so we took some downers and stayed in the Village about six hours. We went to some blues clubs, saw folk rock singer Tim Hardin and went backstage at the Bitter End, did some coke with him there. It was great, like we were all in the same fraternity or something. But when we started to leave it, was as though we were the only ones who were visibly drunk. Drunk-drunk, stumbling-down-the-six-blocks-to-the-loft drunk, stepping over winos passed out on sidewalks, oblivious to anything. Finally, we got to the building. As I fumbled for the keys I realized I didn't have the fucking keys, that Geoff must have the keys, or they must be back at the club, since we'd been using them to hold the gobs of coke we'd been sniffing. We were too wasted to go back to the club. We had no choice; we'd have to go up the fire escape.

I climbed on Geoff's shoulders and he hoisted me up to grab the end of the ladder. After a few tugs, it came creaking down. We were laughing uncontrollably. I leapt up and pulled myself onto the stairs, Geoff right behind me. Up we climbed, up, up. And up. At the fifth floor we stood on the platform, basking in the majesty of it all—starlit New York City, ours for the taking. We could do whatever we wanted, get as fucked up as we pleased, even break ourselves in to our own apartment. We were invincible.

"I have a .38 Special aimed at your stomach," a low, gruff voice warned from out of nowhere, "and if you don't go down immediately I will pull the trigger."

I froze. A curtain flapped at an open window in front of me, revealing a gun barrel glinting in the starlight. Geoff rolled his eyes in disbelief. What could I do? I slumped down and duck-walked across the escape platform, shoved myself past Geoff, and scrambled down the stairs.

We ended up spending the night in Geoff's Volkswagen.

The next morning, the elevator guy took us up to the loft and we fell into our beds. I woke up to ringing in the phone booth. It was Chris Stamp. The Who were still in Australia, he couldn't get me into England yet, but the Who would be coming to the States for a couple of months.

"Tommy," he said, "would you manage the tour?"

Ron Wood
Ann Arbor, 1970

Good-bye Thanks

CHAPTER TWELVE

From: Tom Wright
Sent: Thursday April 06, 2006 4:05 AM
To: Pete Townshend
Subject: good-bye thanks

Hey, when you said you would move a mountain, you didn't have to—Rogan got out of the way on his own. I enjoyed the hospitality. I will be thinking about what you said for a while.

I came over thinking I was gonna arrive, roll up my sleeves, and help you out of a slump. I thought you had lost your drummer and that you would be resurrecting old material that you had passed on decades ago. So it was great to find you on a roll.

When you said, "I can do that stuff in my sleep," I hope that didn't mean it was not worth doing. On the flight over I was getting my thoughts in order so I could say stuff quickly and not waste your time, but as it turned out I didn't say much of anything. I had filmed that Wholigans drummer at the Night of the Living Dead because I love the guy and he is kick-ass and a grown-up warrior on tour with that band around England. The phenomenal thing is that those guys (early 40s) work all over the world with the same gear you toured with prior to *Tommy*, and they have been doing it for years. They all have families, have their own businesses, hire roadies on the spot, and are lucky if they break even. But at soundcheck the other day when they cranked up that new Hiwatt and played "Substitute," I thought I was having a stroke, it was so wonderful. When I was telling you about it and you guys were saying it was too loud to use, I thought I was in the sequel to *Spinal Tap*. Too loud for the Who? I don't think so. The quality I was talking about was not volume at all. It's a sound you had when the Who was white-hot and it did something to one's body.

Anyway, if you are gonna tour as the Who, the first 45 minutes (I think) should be sheer force/excitement/refined grown-up bad ass. Then, if you must, roll out the usual suspects and have a Pete Townshend Presents deal with people who all get along with each

Joe Walsh
at Detroit Rock & Roll Revival

other but who the audience could care less about. This may be the last Who tour, and it was the picture you painted, and lots of people will bring their kids or girlfriends and pay a lot of money to show them what cool really meant. But when the stage fills up with what looks like the wandering millionaires, careful not to step out of line, it just doesn't do it for anybody—I don't care how GOOD they are. My point is if the Wholigans can go out with hardly anything and create excitement, I know you can.

Those martial arts guys who are in their 60s are doing the same things they did when they were 20. The difference is wisdom/finesse/ elegance, and it looks twice as exciting and twice as dangerous as it did when they were 20. They have become masters, a state of conditions that takes a lifetime to achieve. They do not appear suddenly juggling oranges and saying of that other shit, "I can do it in my sleep . . . and I don't want to bore myself . . . but give me your hundred dollars anyway."

Anyway, I was working on the plane with words to STEP TWINS and even when I found out you were kicking out new material I couldn't stop working and it changed every time I tried to copy it over. So now I have words all through my luggage, and even if it kills me I am gonna send you at least one page of them when I get home. Must run. I went up to Norwich and saw Tim and Nick and scared them to death.

All the best, Pete. You are the master of the Who myth; show it one last time for 45 minutes a night.

Love and thanks,

Tom

From: Pete Townshend
Sent: Thursday, April 06, 2006 5:16 AM
To: Tom Wright
Subject: Re: good-bye thanks

Tom. Good to see you too. Glad you survived.

I don't have any time to reply properly to your email. I'm so sorry. But I'll give it 15 minutes. It seems to me that's about what you gave me.

Maybe it's time you stopped worrying about me, and what I might do right and wrong, and look at your own record. You have a fabulous inheritance of photographic artifacts, memories, experience, and are really funny when you write and talk. You are right to say that the world is in a strange way, and it is folks like us that failed to do anything to change the way it was headed. Make something that bears your name and tells the truth. I am Tom Wright. Etc.

At least music and words can inspire, that's all old folks can do. You have to realize that you and I began to classify as Old Folks as soon as we turned 25. I think you came to rock 'n' roll as a religion a little late. The Who are treated by some of their fans as though they were the

Tom Wright
backstage at the Grande, 1969

Big City baseball team—always about to claw back and make their fans happy and proud again.

When Keith Moon stopped wisecracking about me being a grouch and faced the fact he was going to die, it was too late. He took a friendship and a musical dynamic with him that cannot be replaced by some younger dude with no brain who thinks all he has to do is throw sticks at me to make me jump. We have no band. Keith died. From that day forward, when Roger became the one who suddenly decided that Keith had always been his greatest friend and musical ally (and was thus irreplaceable except by some clone), it became clear that we would never, ever move forward. We would always be stuck in a time warp, trying to relive something that could never be lived except by parody bands pretending they took the same path. But they don't take our path. They miss out the best part of it. The part I did in private mostly.

While Keith was frying his brain, and you were building a life somewhere, usually I was working. I worked so fucking hard I went crazy. And what I delivered was never, ever enough. Never enough for Roger, never enough for fans, and never enough for the future. I've got used to people wanting more from me and I have stopped worrying about it.

I can help you with what it is you want to do, or should I say what it is I believe you should want to do. But the longer you look at me, and hope for me to complete the circle for you, the longer you delay your own journey.

If the message you felt charged to send me was that I should blow what's left of my hearing out simply to make the right "Who" sound, you should be ashamed. You were there when I made that noise. So cherish that. Also cherish the fact that I am alive and happy, and when I was a kid, I brought pleasure to millions of people. Cherish the fact that I was able to do that partly because you came into my life when I was young and unformed, and your function was to get me high and play me Jimmy Reed records. I did the rest, Tom, with help only from Kit and Chris. No one else helped. NO ONE. The creative process makes its own way driven by insecurity, disease, low self-esteem, anger, and the need for money. Sick fucks like the kid from Nirvana called all that shit "passion" then put a gun in his mouth. It can feel like passion, but we were like assault troops in a war where there was no enemy but ourselves.

What I am trying to do today is simply enjoy every day.

Pete

From: Pete Townshend
Sent: Thursday, April 06, 2006 12:48 PM
To: Tom Wright
Subject: Re: good-bye thanks

Tom, a little more now the studio day is behind me.

I actually enjoy every day—most days. That is an achievement for me.

But looking at what you've been through, what is most important for me to say is that anything I can do to help you make a good book deal, a movie, a documentary, or even a radio show, I will gladly do.

If you need me to back you up (maybe with your agent), I'll do so.

If you need studio resources, cameras, lights, action, etc., it's all here for you. A great time to come back to the UK to make a film (possibly with Matt helping) would be after the tour, so next spring. In the meantime, we could knock up a presentation treatment and sell it to VH1.

On the back of your hit VH1 rock story show, "Tom Wright: The Inventor of Grande Ballroom Panic Syndrome," you can then spend your twilight years touring rock conventions telling people where I went wrong in 1989 by wearing a Baggy Suit.

Pete

*Pete Townshend
1967*

the front door," he said. Bob had a white, re-glued Fender Strat with an electric short. It would have to do.

A tall, redheaded guy came in from the side door, his face colored with clown paint. Scary. "I'm Dave Miller," he said. "I'm the announcer." He walked over to Pete and handed him a joint. "It's a pretty good crowd," he said, "but then it's like this every Friday."

"Bloody hell," said Pete, taking a big hit and holding it in.

"Could you get us a drink?" asked Keith, sounding like Peter O'Toole addressing the Queen's butler.

"Fuck no," Dave said, laughing. "We don't have alcohol here. I'll announce you, and then you come out."

The band formed a line behind Dave at the stage door. He got the last of the joint from Pete and then stepped out on the stage. "Okay," he said, looking out over the crowd, "let's"—he gave a you're-gonna-love-this grin— "welcome the Who-o-o-o!"

Bob handed Pete the guitar at the doorway, the band scrambled to their spots. My stomach tightened. The stage was about chest high. People rested their elbows on it. No cops, no security. Just wall-to-wall humanity, waiting to rock. A loud crackle came from Pete's guitar as he jammed the lead into the amp socket. Like a machine gun, they kicked off "Substitute." Wow.

"Jonesy, look at this!" I shouted. "They're singing with the band. They know the song!" This had never happened in the States. The crowd was pulsing like a well-trained combat unit. Guys were banging their heads and hands on the stage.

The band looked at each other. This was the audience they'd worked their whole lives to find, and halfway into the first song they knew it for sure. The entire building seemed to work with them. The crowd, stoned out of their minds, was watching, approving everything the band did. It was as if this whole tour had been a long, agonizing foot race to this, the last lap, with no one behind them. The guys got their second wind from the roar of the crowd and went full blast. For the Who, it was the perfect set.

The next day they would sell a zillion records in Detroit, disc jockeys raving. The Who had finally arrived in America . . . moments before they were ready to leave and never come back.

They never topped that show.

Birthday Greetings

CHAPTER FOURTEEN

Pete Townshend
1967

From: Tom Wright
Sent: May 18, 2006
To: Pete Townshend
Subject: Birthday Greetings

Hello Pete,

Happy birthday!

If I had been more organized and remembered, I would've made you another copy of the two-tape biography of Frank Lloyd Wright, seeing as how the first one wound up in the sweaty palms of the Plaza hotel concierge guy, the '02 tour. The documentary is fascinating from the first minute. But way toward the end, when he turned 70, he began his most wondrous projects. His mind was in high gear and he was thinking clearer than in his whole life. He was beginning construction on the Guggenheim, he had a huge studio, house, and intern quarters in the middle of Arizona, and an even bigger compound/estate in Wisconsin, nestled on a hill overlooking a river, miles and miles from the nearest neighbor. He was making money. He'd outlived most of his scandals and tragic moments and was married to a gorgeous Russian woman a third his age. She took care of everything. It was such an uplifting life. He worked up until he was 93 or 94. Then in the middle of a handful of huge projects, he had stomach pains, was rushed to the hospital, and died a couple of days later.

So, since I think that you are yet to do your most lasting work—your masterpieces—I wanted you to see it. When they announced your birthday on the radio today and said you were a whopping 61, I regretted not running you another copy. What I said about your work to come downplays your early work, of course. *Tommy* was a masterpiece of an era. Actually, it was an Amazing Journey. It showed a lot of people that things could be complex, deep, yet the music could still be exciting. An entire generation has that album burned into their gray cells. It's a youthful masterwork. But most everything up to this point has been boot camp, including *Tommy.* Now that you're an expert in blues, pop, rock, jazz, folk, knowledgeable of the whole world of classics and orchestral arrangements, I just see this all coming together in a mature way, in the way that the Guggenheim is a statement to all of mankind. Bits and pieces from life's everywhere, utilized and built into something that is new and old at the same time. That, most importantly, shows by example a spiritual future.

I know, I know—I'm not to worry about that kind of stuff. And I don't. You are set, old man, no doubt about it. Since it's your birthday, I just wanted to say that the best is yet to come. And from over here, it looks like everything is right on time.

I'm back at the window with all those recent memories. I've rolled everything over and over in my head, and probably just about now have things committed to permanent brain files.

After I left your place, Pridden drove me downtown and dropped me off at the train station headed for Norwich. After I figured out how to use the pay phones, I got Andy Neil on the phone and asked him to find a number and address for Tim Bartlett in Norwich. I would ride up to Norwich and call him from there. We are talking sheer bravado here. Tim didn't know I was coming, and I didn't know how to contact him. I wouldn't get to Norwich until seven; I planned to say hello and take the 9 o'clock back to London.

The train ride to Norwich had a calming effect, like I was escaping the Third World. Rolling through countryside that grew more picturesque and lush with every mile, under gentle pockets of rain and sunshine. At the station in Norwich, I got Andy back on the phone; he gave me some numbers for Tim, then said, "You just stepped in it, mate. Tim's mum died yesterday and the family's coming in from everywhere. The funeral's tomorrow. Tim is 70 miles away at his father's house, but he wants you to call him on his cell."

Once he was sure it was really me on the phone, Tim chewed me out for not telling him I was coming. "Forty-five years without a word, and now you're in Norwich just as I'm planning my mother's funeral. Your timing is as jolting as ever." He wasn't really pissed off or anything, just wanted to rattle me for rattling him. He seemed to get mad for real, though, when I told him I was leaving at 9 because I had a film shoot the next day in London. I think I told you that some filmmakers that Andy knew were doing a documentary on Iggy Pop and the Stooges and wanted to ask me about Iggy and Detroit on camera, even though I'd told them I thought the guy was a loser and I hated his music except for "1969" and that he was nothing but trouble and confusion whenever he played the Grande. If it weren't for the fact that John Sinclair's people were writing glowing reports and getting them published—reports that were all bullshit—nobody would ever have paid any attention to this guy's goofy approach to the Grande: rolling around on the stage smearing peanut butter on himself and sticking his tongue out at the audience while they booed him and threw Cokes and ice from paper cups. Then the review that Sinclair's people would send out would say everybody loved it and went wild 'cause Iggy was so cosmic. I'd told Andy this, he'd told the filmmaker, and the guy still wanted to do it. I'd committed to it and it was gonna happen the next day, so I couldn't stay in Norwich. Or so I thought.

I let Tim talk me into staying. He would leave when he hung up the phone, he told me, but he had to pick up his youngest brother who was flying in from Singapore. Soonest he could meet me was at 10 o'clock. So I walked aimlessly around one of the most beautiful little towns in England—cobblestone streets, high-tech shops next to 1,000 year old churches, pubs with people inside singing and laughing, boats still moving on a river through town. It had stopped raining just as I walked out of the train station; the sky was clearing for one of those puffy cloud sunsets that seem so British. Everything was still wet and glistened and shined. I felt like I could have stayed forever.

Tim met me at an inn with his sister and brother and insisted on buying a bottle of champagne and turned down the first one they brought. He insisted they bring a such-and-such, cost him thirty-five pounds. Ouch. He looks pretty much the same, but with real short hair and tiny eyeglasses. He wore a well-worn leather Ralph Lauren kind of suit jacket and jeans; he looked really cool. But it turns out that he thinks that when I got kicked out of England, I crushed his dreams of forming a band with Cam and me. He reminded me that we were good when we ran out of money and played the sidewalks in Normandy . . . and actually made some money. He said because of all the records and since Cam was so good-looking and could actually sing and play guitar that we could've been a real group. I couldn't believe what I was hearing; because I got kicked out of the country, I ruined his shot at being in a band and having a life of rock-stardom. Can you imagine? I can't. I told him I thanked God on a regular basis for never letting me in a band or have money in my hand. "Tim, I would've died years ago if we were in a band. Cyril Davies was my hero; he died onstage, remember? I actually thought that was cool. No, I am so grateful that I never got locked into a band or a company or a career or a business because, at one point, I could have afforded to kill myself. And I would have. Besides, I couldn't really play more than a few chords and I have a terrible twangy voice."

But we kept talking about Sunnyside Road, Ealing, Ibiza, and Formentera, and, finally, at 2 AM, Tim helped me find a small but expensive hotel. The next morning we met for breakfast and walked to the train station. I took the 9 o'clock back to London, and, without changing clothes, went straight to the film shoot.

I can't wait to see the playbacks. Here I was talking to some guy who wasn't even old enough to go to school when the Grande was going, and all he knew about Detroit was Motown, the MC5, and Iggy Stooge. Everything he thought he knew was all wrong and based on old PR pieces as history. The interview went on for two hours. I was on a roll and articulated, I think, a pretty clear picture of the Grande. At least, how cutting edge it all was, how just staying alive and out of jail while getting high and putting on concerts was an exciting and full-time job.

It had all the revolutionary spirit of the Crusades and World War II combined. Anyway, I hope to get my copy any day now, and I will get it transcribed.

The day after that I flew back to Toronto, spent the night with friends, and then drove to Michigan the next day. I spent a few days unwinding at home, then took off driving my mom to Texas. I'd promised her the trip. She'd been packed and ready to go down for the winter back in October, but I'd derailed that plan with the surprise heart attack.

First stop was Russ Schlagbaum's down in Ohio. We spent the night there, and in the morning we all had breakfast, his daughter included. He's excited about working on the Who tour, has been spinning his wheels since not going back with the Stones. From there we drove to Birmingham, stayed with family, left the day after that for Texas and made it all the way to Corsicana, about an hour's drive south of Dallas. The only reason I stopped there was because I was tired and it was getting dark, but what a great place. An undiscovered part of Texas. Nothing was renovated yet. Just an old town, well-maintained, kind of the Mexican version of Norwich with a few cowboys wandering around or driving by in pickups, Tex-Mex food like you wouldn't believe. I could have stayed there forever. We drove on to Austin and eventually made it to San Antonio, stayed for a few days, saw everybody we knew for fifteen minutes apiece, then drove all the way back. 4,553 miles on the meter.

I've been home a couple of weeks, signed the book contract, and started to write. I was gonna make some headway with it so I can see the "Who's Left" tour in Switzerland and Austria. Right after those two shows I have to get to L.A. and catch the week of James Gang rehearsals. I wanna be there for the first note and eventually shoot some new pictures for them, plus, I almost forgot, I wanna show Joe a song, "Run Jesse Run." I started it in '82 and it was gonna be about Jesse Jackson, but he rapidly turned stupid and I stopped messing with it but, wow, the *James Gang Rides Again* . . . again. Everybody looks good. It won't be like the Cream thing with ambulances and oxygen tanks.

Anyway, I told you I was gonna think about all the neat stuff we talked about and how I needed to put up or shut up. But stuff happens. Like your birthday. I hope it is the best one you ever had. It could be worse—you could be as old as me.

Love, Tom

From: Pete Townshend
Sent: Friday, May 19, 2006
To: Tom Wright
Subject: Re: Birthday Greetings

What a great birthday present. A story . . . thank you so much. I look
forward to seeing you again as soon as it can happen.

Pete

Colombian dancer
San Antonio

Super Glue and Cherry Bombs

Traveling with Keith Moon was like knowing that the fuse was lit—and the clock was ticking.

It wasn't all pranks. There were stories, amazingly hilarious stories. And there was drinking, lots and lots of drinking. Keith took so much speed he never really got drunk, while everybody else would need stretchers. And on the tour bus, Keith would always need to stop for something. Kmarts when we could find them, but usually it'd be a clump of stores near the truck stops. While we gassed up the bus, he'd buy clothes, toothpaste and a toothbrush, dry shampoo. Keith had discovered that he could stay up all night, spray this "dry shampoo" stuff on his hair, rub it with a towel, and look good to go for another day. When you saw Keith, you never knew if he'd been up all night or was actually showered, shampooed, and rested.

To Pete, I'd introduced pot. To Keith, it was Super Glue and cherry bombs, which, in his hands, became fiendish tools of mayhem and practical jokes. And it'd all started out so innocently.

One day on the bus, I was repairing a camera bag strap. I clamped the strap with a couple of clothespins and Keith was transfixed. Not hard when you're riding across the Corn Belt in an old Greyhound with lumber bunks and a malodorous bathroom.

Keith stood up to get a closer look. "What is that?" he asked.

"Super Glue," I said.

Keith's eyes got wide. "Soooooooooper Glue," he whispered, like I'd passed on a secret code.

Did I stop things right there? Hell, no. Idiot.

"This stuff dries in seconds," I told him. "If you get it on your fingers, they'll stick together and nothing but time or razor blades can break you loose. It'll glue almost anything to anything."

Pete Townshend
1967

I'm convinced that from then on, at every stop on the road, Keith purchased as much Super Glue as he could find. Lucky for us, he didn't feel the need to sabotage the bus. It was the hotels that caught most of the early experimentation. Like using Super Glue on the back of the hotel artwork, making those cheesy poster-print landscapes permanently, immutably crooked. From there, Keith moved on to gluing the plastic toilet seats to their porcelain bowls. And then there were the washrags he glued to the wall or the floor. He'd wet them so they'd look as if they'd just been tossed; the cleaning crew would need blowtorches to get the stuff up. Keith's favorite? Just before we'd check out, he'd glue the telephone receiver in place.

In all cases, since we were miles down the road before his shenanigans were discovered, I never found out about a lot of the hotel stuff until after the tour, when the bills came pouring into the travel agency. There was even an invoice for redoing an entire ceiling; what appeared to be a glass of urine was "somehow attached to the ceiling above the entrance door." Later, I read in a book that in London Keith had managed to secure pieces of furniture to the ceiling. I can't vouch for that, but if it indeed happened, no doubt Super Glue was involved.

Keith Moon
1968

Keith's discovery of cherry bombs was the result of my trying to protect his hands. Really. We were somewhere in the Deep South and pulled into a truck stop to gas up the bus. While we were waiting, we wandered into the huge fireworks store nearby. It was like a giant supermarket, filled with every kind of firework you could imagine: Roman candles, bottle rockets the size of mortar shells, and, in what should have been the produce section, cherry bombs.

"Look!" Keith said. "I've never seen so many bangers in me life!"

"Oh, no," I told him, "those aren't bangers," the lame British-style fireworks that make a little bang like a cap gun and nine times out of ten go off in your hand. Keith was right, though: American cherry bombs did look just like English bangers.

"A cherry bomb is like a mini stick of dynamite," I explained. "If it goes off in your hand, you'll definitely lose some fingers. And get this, you can throw it in water and it won't go out. When I was twelve we used to make our own hand grenades with cement or clay wrapped around cherry bombs. We were going strong that summer until the neighbor's dog got hurt when we tried to blow up their garbage can. Then in high school, some guy blew up a toilet with one. Seriously, Keith," I warned, "you could get hurt with those."

I thought I'd just saved an Englishman's hands. Of course, what I'd actually done was doom every bathroom we used from the Carolinas to Manhattan. While I helped Bob Pridden purchase several cases of smoke bombs, Keith slipped John some cash to buy a case of cherry bombs. From then on, every time we stopped to eat or shop, Keith's last move was to run back to use the john. Level the john, was more like it. He'd light a cherry bomb, toss it into the toilet, and flush. He'd still have a couple of seconds to make it out the door before a massive thud rumbled the ground and water began to spout from where the toilet used to be. By the time he jumped back on the bus, we were zooming on down the road not knowing a thing—other than Keith was always the last one on.

When we finally got to New York, we checked into the Gorham Hotel, where Keith secretly offloaded his supplies of Super Glue and cherry bombs. I was the road manager, and now that we were in New York the real managers, who were in town, took over. They'd set up press conferences, and there was a *Life* magazine photo shoot in the morning in Central Park using a big Union Jack.

After the *Life* session and lunch, I went down to the front desk to make sure that the band, all staying on the twelfth floor, wouldn't be disturbed. I also asked if anyone knew why Mr. Moon wasn't answering his phone. "Well, you're calling the wrong room," said the guy behind the desk. "Mr. Moon's on the fourteenth floor. He asked to be moved right after you checked them all in yesterday."

No big deal, I thought, Keith probably wants the total New York City experience—the higher up, the better, right? I couldn't have been more wrong.

Keith had been busy. Unbeknownst to anyone, he'd planted a few unlit cherry bombs in the standup ashtrays in the hotel hallways and Super Glued a set of elevator doors closed—just one, not all, so it seemed like a freak accident rather than a prank—before returning to his room. Now he was looking out his open window, watching pedestrians scurry like ants beneath the city's skyscrapers. At just the strategic moment, he'd light a cherry bomb with his cigarette and then hurl it from his window onto rush-hour traffic fourteen stories below. The bomb would go off in the air about sixty feet above the suits and ties with briefcases, most of whom would hit the deck at the explosion. It was high drama, which was always so much fun for Keith.

Eventually, the suits would get up and readjust, the traffic light would change, and everyone would move on. If Keith was patient for a half-hour or so, he could lob another one. Between bombs, he'd revisit all the ashtrays, placing lit cigarettes in them that would slowly burn their way toward the tip of the cherry bomb fuse.

The ashtray on the second floor, just above the lobby, was the first to blow. Thinking they were under attack, the front desk immediately called the police, who arrived in minutes with guns drawn. The cops tried the elevator, but Keith had taken care of that. So they dashed up the stairs, surrounding in a very official way the smoldering bits of the demolished ashtray. It was determined that someone had just shot the ashtray; the cops phoned for backup. Just as a fleet of black-and-whites screeched to a siren-screaming halt in front of the hotel, Keith lobbed another cherry bomb, which exploded fifty feet above the cop cars.

Now Keith was banging on my door. I'd just stepped out of the shower and was clueless.

"I say, have you seen what's happening?" he exclaimed as he rushed into the room. He opened my window and leaned out. "I think somebody's been shot!"

I hadn't heard a thing, I told him, and went back into the bathroom to dry off and get dressed. Apparently, the cops had sent a couple of guys across the street to see where the shots were coming from. Keith stepped back from the window. He'd be right back, he yelled to me, he was heading down to the bar to find out what was going on.

Oh, and just to keep it interesting, he lit another cherry bomb, tossed it out my window, and popped out of the room, closing the door behind him.

That, I did hear.

I ran to the window. Two cops were sprinting toward the hotel, yelling to other cops. They seemed to have things under control, so I closed the window and turned on the TV, and then wandered back into the bathroom to shave. Suddenly, there was banging on my door. It had to be Keith, I thought. Nobody in his right mind would knock that loud.

When I swung open the door I found myself staring at more gun barrels than I'd ever seen in my life—especially ones pointed at me. There were guys laying flat on the hall floor, shotguns aimed at my crotch; there were guys flat up against both hallway walls, and there was a big gang of guys standing face-to-face with me, pistols pointed at my chest.

"Where's the piece?! Where's the piece?!" the cop closest to me yelled.

Instinctively, I raised my hands, just like in the movies.

"The piece! Where's the piece?!" he yelled again.

I honestly had no idea what he was talking about. "P-piece?" I managed to stammer. "Piece of what?"

"The gun, asshole!" he roared. "Where's the gun?!"

It was at times like these, when Keith wasn't there, that you thought about him anyway. It took five minutes of yelling, searching, pleading, and explaining to make clear to them that I'd just gotten out of the shower and had not a clue as to what was going on.

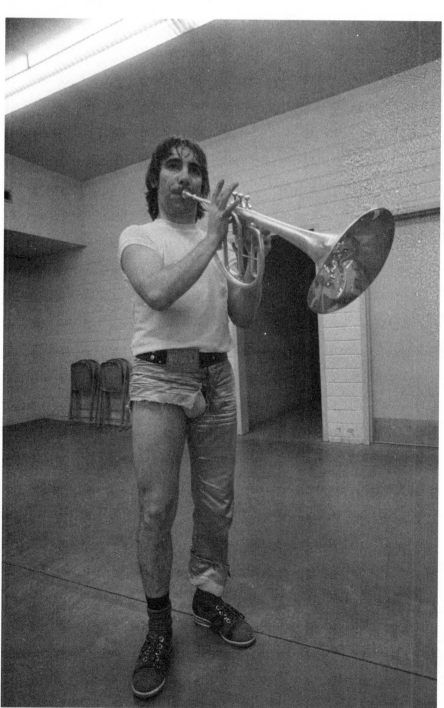

Keith Moon
Dallas, Texas, 1971

Pete Townshend
1967

Then Keith strolled in. He was dressed in a silk smoking jacket, puffing a cigarette from a long, elegant holder. He introduced himself and shook each cop's hand. He even signed an album for the cop head honcho. When the police left, they thought they'd been in the company of a young David Niven.

I sat down, bewildered as to what had just happened, and opened a beer. Then it hit me.

Cherry bombs.

Not only do American cherry bombs look like English bangers, they also resemble smoke bombs—the red ones, anyway. Smoke bombs came in M&M candy colors, most of them red, but there were a few greens and yellows. After the Gorham fiasco, I hoped that it hadn't occurred to Keith to slide a few cherry bombs into the box of smoke bombs that Bob used occasionally onstage. Bob was good; he'd light them behind, or roll them under, the amps, and it'd look like a complex electrical fire. Swapping smoke bombs for cherry bombs—now that was just too scary to worry about, and if I brought it up, it would happen for certain, so I kept my mouth shut and tried to forget about it.

The next gig was somewhere in New Jersey, on the boardwalk. Rumor was that the place was run by the mob. A beautiful club, but not a rock hall. The Who's gig was to be a first, a Sunday afternoon matinee. Something for the kids.

When we got there, we found the building was huge, built right up to the boardwalk, on stilts above the Atlantic's edge. The exterior looked like a huge post office from the 1940s, but inside it was all renovated, clean as a whistle. Pridden went to work, rolling equipment up onto the stage. I liked to watch Bob. The stage was his canvas and he'd set the gear up as perfect as a painting.

From out of nowhere, two big hulks in shiny suits appeared and walked up to him.

"How you doing, guy?" the first one asked. "You work with the band, do ya? Well, just so there's no misunderstanding in your mind, we want to point out that this here stage is brand-fucking-new. Management doesn't want it scratched up and asked us to make a special trip and let you know this. Just so you know."

I was downwind of the gangster clones, but close enough to see that both of these guys had guns under their suit coats. And they wanted Bob to see them. They ignored me. I was glad; I got the picture.

"We'll come back after the show and check the stage together," the guy told Bob. "Your name again? Bobby? Okay, Bobby, you tell your boys no nicks, cuts, or bruises on this floor."

The goons walked off the stage and disappeared in the dark end of the hall.

This was no joke, I told Bob. Those guys mean business. It was Jersey, for Christ's sake, and those guys weren't disc jockeys. I knew this could end up ugly.

The band showed up an hour late for the two o'clock soundcheck and played a couple of songs that sounded great. Keith had trouble with his tom-tom sliding away from him, the one item that Bob usually nailed directly to the floor.

"We can't muck up the floor," Bob explained to Keith, "or a couple of guys in suits may break my legs or shoot me. I'll gaffer tape the tom and it'll be fine."

I joined Bob in trying to impress upon Keith the real gravity of the situation. Deep down, I knew it was a terrible mistake—but I tried anyway.

"Keith, this is a gangster place," I said, doing my best to get him to understand. "Can't you tell? Run-down and funky on the outside, ten zillion bucks on the inside? This is their party place, and I promise they are dead serious. We cannot mess up their floor, Keith. Pridden already told you that if the toms move, he'll crawl back and hold them."

Then I explained things to Pete, that the thug brothers had heard the band breaks up their gear and they'd dropped by to let us know—guns and all—exactly what the company policy was. I got eye-to-eye promises from both Keith and Pete that they'd tone it down. Townshend said he'd play a Rickenbacker, the easiest to destruct of his guitars, for "My Generation," and that he'd "just jam it down on the mic-stand base and it'll blow up like a light bulb, no problem."

Well, there was a problem. No Rickenbacker. He'd demolished it a couple of weeks before and nobody had even thought to get another one. He'd have to use the solid, sturdy Fender. "Well, I'll just bang the guitar into the speaker cabinets," Pete said. "Don't worry, Tom, you're so damn paranoid. We're not going to change our show for two guys in suits. We come from the land of suits. Remember?"

At just after four, the band started up to a packed house of mostly fourteen-year-olds. The Who sounded just right, the way they did whenever they had three days without a show. Fresh, strong. Loud and crystal-clear. Soon,

Pete Townshend
1967

Keith was soaked with sweat; Pete, too. If the place had air-conditioning, management must've shut it off when the crowd arrived.

The band kicked off "My Generation" with a vengeance. Halfway through, Keith was getting dangerously mad over his tom-toms; they kept rocking, almost falling over backwards, every time he banged them. Pridden, crouched behind the guitar amp, ready to light a handful of smoke bombs, was no help.

Meanwhile, Roger had just zeroed in on two guys in suits who were standing below the stage, in the orchestra pit. Daltrey was swinging the mic stand down, trying to hit them with it. They were trying to grab the mic stand, no doubt to pull Rodge down off the stage and beat him to death with it. Nobody had told Roger what was up, and today, in front of all that jail bait—or "veal," as Entwistle called the underage lassies—here he was, going for an Oscar by trying to scare some grown-ups.

Not to be outdone, Townshend started swinging his Fender guitar like a baseball bat, slamming the wood floor in what looked like a desperate attempt to save some kid trapped under the stage. Then Keith spotted the thug brothers and hurled cymbals and stands down into the orchestra pit. He ripped up the huge tom-tom, slammed it on the gleaming oak floor a couple of times, and then picked it up over his head and heaved it directly at the two goons who were headed full-steam through the veal toward the stage stairs.

Keith looked so crazed that I was now more scared of him than the hit men. Pete finished off his guitar, now nothing but a pile of splinters and wires, and stalked off the stage as if he was disgusted by the whole world.

Just as the goons reached the stairs, the smoke bombs went off. But of course, they weren't smoke bombs. Thank you, Keith Moon.

The crack of munitions was not a popular sound with that crowd. The whole building froze.

Keith took the opportunity to run for his life. He sprinted full-force through the fire exit door, tripping the brand-new fire alarm, tore through a crowd gathered on the boardwalk, hopped up onto the railing, and jumped straight down like he was bailing out of a burning plane.

He might as well have been.

The boardwalk was a good forty feet above the ocean. With the rail and Keith's upward trajectory, it was a fifty-foot drop, easy. Pridden ran to the boardwalk, yelling, "He can't swim! He can't swim!" So now a gang of teenage wannabe heroes pulled off their shirts and shoes and started jumping in. Cops swarmed from all sides. A jeep ambulance appeared down on the rocky beach, while lifeguards worked on pulling kids out of the chilly water. Someone finally spotted Keith, hanging motionless on a pier pole. Once sure that Moon was alive, Bob ran back to the stage and started hurriedly rolling stuff onto the rent-a-truck.

On my way down to the ambulance, I passed the dressing room. Entwistle was wiping off his bass, telling Pete he thought it'd been a good show. Pete agreed.

And though Keith wasn't there at that moment, I thought about him anyway.

CHAPTER SIXTEEN

The Albert

New York City's Albert Hotel was a secret. Muddy Waters could tell you about it. Bob Dylan could tell you about it. The Moby Grape could make a mini-series on it. It was at University Place and 11th, pretty big, just a short walk from Washington Square Park, about thirty blocks from classy hotels and about ten blocks from the really shitty ones. The Albert was about fifty years past her prime; at one time posh, when I got there it was rundown and cheap. It had roughly twenty floors and didn't really look that bad from the outside, all granite and stone. It was the seedy characters wandering the sidewalk that gave it away.

Bob Dylan used to practice there, but when I lived there in 1968, after I'd road-managed the Who's first headlining U.S. tour, it was folk rock singer Tim Hardin in the basement. But mostly it was Moby Grape, the psychedelic rockers from California. They'd play nonstop from ten at night 'til eight in the morning. I'd fall asleep on the tenth floor and could hear them through my pillow. They were so good you couldn't sleep, though their god-awful records belied this. They would take a riff and just keep playing and varying it from within, stretching it, expanding it. By the time they got to the recording studio, though, they'd have been up for so many days that they forgot what was good about the song. At the Albert, nobody cared what their records sounded like, because at night, if you got real quiet at your place and lay down, you could hear them in the basement. And nine times out of ten it'd be great, and sometimes it would be the greatest music you'd ever heard. Seriously.

Moby Grape eventually got the ol' heave-ho from the basement. One morning around 4 AM, as the all-night rehearsal jam in the bowels of the building was still going strong—and sounding great—the Pakistani desk clerk showed up, stopping one of the Grape's hour-long song jams in mid-flight. Incensed, Skip Spence, the Grape's frontman, yanked off his guitar and chased the tiny refugee gripping a flashlight back up the dark wooden staircase to the lobby. On the way, Spence slowed down long enough to smash the glass on a firebox that held an extinguisher and an axe.

Austin, 1976

Unlike Moon, Spence chose the axe, ripping it from its mooring with his right hand, which was now bleeding profusely, and continued the chase. Just as he reached the lobby, the crazed, stoned longhair clutching a shiny axe dripping with blood ran right into a neighborhood beat cop who'd happened by as the terrified desk clerk fled the building. Spence left in handcuffs after a gaggle of squad cars screeched to a halt in the front of the Albert, the cops expecting a pile of dead bodies. I never heard or saw Moby Grape again.

Maître d', Albert Hotel
New York City, 1976

Since the Albert was in the gray area, it was hard to book. No wandering family of tourists would ever just stroll by, and it was too expensive for bums and people who were actually broke for real. So the management let rooms to selected renegades—certain musicians, hookers (if they were beautiful and discreet), drug salesmen, artists, gangsters. It was a long process to get in. I moved in with Geoff, the Blues Magoos drummer. It'd taken a month of cajoling, but we finally got the "presidential suite": three bedrooms, a sitting room, kitchen, two bathrooms, a banquet room, plus a living room with a fireplace for $700 a month. We moved in and repainted everything, had the whole place recarpeted.

The Who were off touring the U.K. yet again. For the time being, I was stuck in New York, getting some work as a fashion and rock photographer. At the Albert, I built a massive darkroom in the master bedroom and bathroom, and put in a fifteen-foot stainless steel sink that'd come out of

CHAPTER SEVENTEEN

The Grande

For destitute hillbillies, blacks, and immigrants, Detroit was the promised land of jobs, jobs, and more jobs. For young guys my age, it looked like a breeding ground for robots. A huge, dirty, mechanized world divided into eight-hour shifts, nothing to look forward to, but sweat, bondage, old age, and cancer. Turns out, everybody was right.

In Detroit, the urge to be different became the demand. Kids there knew from birth the strength and power of the group strike. Now, these kids were ready to join forces because the enemy was so obvious. It was simply Them.

In other cities, everyone was sneaking around smoking pot. In Detroit, they were rolling joints on the street. They went after pot-smoking like it was baseball, and at that time, there was more music per square inch in Detroit than anywhere in the country. So what started as the idealistic musical dream of beat poets and entrepreneurs on the West Coast surfaced in Detroit as assembly-line revolt, the birthplace and nursery for heavy metal. And the Grande Ballroom was the hatchery.

The Grande was special. It'd opened a year or so before the stock market crash, and from pictures found in its basement, you could see it'd once been suitable for royalty—all roses, white linen tablecloths, ball gowns, and tuxedos. All the big orchestras played there, including Louis Armstrong. Detroit had a lot of elegant ballrooms, many of them bigger, but the Grande was the last one built from that era of grand occasions, when weekends in a factory town meant elegance and élan.

By the 1950s, the neighborhoods near the Grande were ghettos, and the ballroom was boarded up, braced for the apocalypse. Soon, a slumlord who'd been buying up recently ghetto-ized properties bought the Grande at auction and rented the upstairs on weekends as a black skating rink. The

Ted Nugent and
the Amboy Dukes
Farmington, Michigan, 1970

Russ Gibb
Grande founder, radio deejay, and teacher, 1968

oak dance floor held up, but everything else in the building was trashed. Eventually the landlord boxed up hundreds of roller skates in the basement, kicked everyone out, and hung plywood over all the windows and doors, inside and out. Nothing happened for ten years.

In the late '60s, Russ Gibb, a full-time high school teacher and part-time radio deejay, unshuttered the ballroom and brought music back to the Grande.

The shows were designed to nail your ass to the wall. Julie Driscoll, Joe Cocker, and Chuck Berry in one night. You knew as soon as you saw that lineup that you could get as high as you wanted and wouldn't be let down. Russ was canny, and he knew how to book the place. By the time I arrived, he'd been all over England, had met the major booking agents and told them, "Look, you've got the band playing New York and California. All you have to do is stop in Detroit. You've already paid for the flight, and the band can stay in people's houses at no cost." Cream played three nights and crashed with different people each night, sleeping on the floor.

We kept three uniformed Detroit cops working the Grande. One was in the parking lot to make sure nobody got shot. Another was indoors by the ticket booth, making sure we didn't get robbed. And the third stayed in the office, trying not to upset anyone. Our relationship with the cops was a standoff. Everyone at the Grande was either high or getting high and not apologizing. And the cops knew it. But we were paying the cops. Bottom line, it was an unspoken agreement. We wouldn't blow smoke in their faces, and they wouldn't come looking to shake everyone down.

In Detroit, the MC5, aka the Motor City Five, was the dope-smokers' antidote for factory noise. For $200 a night they were the house band at the Grande. They were never truly captured on record and some of the band members—guitarists Wayne Kramer and Fred "Sonic" Smith, bassist Michael Davis, drummer Dennis Thompson, and frontman Rob Tyner— eventually wound up going to prison or becoming junkies. Their legacy will probably confuse the historians, but for two solid years, they exposed

MC5 basement rehearsal
Ann Arbor, 1968

thousands of factory rats to spine-chilling rock and roll, public pot-smoking, profanity, and revolutionary camaraderie. Outside of blazing machine guns in your face, this was about as exciting as anyone could stand—and twice as loud.

When you did anything in Detroit, you did it for eight hours. Fishing, breaking in a new girlfriend, working on your car, rehearsing the band— you did it for eight hours at a time. This was a fact of life. So if you were in the MC5 and booked to play at the Grande in three weeks, it meant that you'd put a minimum of 120 hours of rehearsal time into a forty-minute set. The girls would make your stage clothes; the roadies would repair all the tubes and wires and repaint all the sound gear in new flat black. And the band would churn out each song hundreds of times against a stopwatch until it was as easy as breathing. An MC5 set's flight pattern was like a rocket—no pauses, no wavers, no hesitation. Floor it, and risk everything.

So while the English bands like Traffic or Clapton sat in one dressing room rearranging their floppy hats and scarves, the MC5 was in the other washing down black mollies with wine, passing huge joints, and doing deep-knee bends in a huddle, while their manager—Detroit poet and White Panther Party leader John Sinclair—kept the joints lit.

"What are we gonna do out there?" Sinclair would yell.

"Kill 'em!" was always the group reply.

"Who's gonna blow those English fags off the stage?"

"We are!"

The whole band would be running in place at this point, breaking a sweat, John still working them over.

"Who's the baddest, highest, get-down motherfuckers?" Sinclair'd yell.

"The *Five!*" they'd roar like commandos about to bail out on a suicide mission.

When John got the okay, he'd take the stage, flash the peace sign, light up a joint, and bellow into the mic like a wild man, "*The . . . M . . . Ceee . . . Fiiive!*" The band would scramble to the stage like snorting, raging bulls turned loose in a Borden's dairy, Tyner screaming, "Kick out the jams, motherfuckers!"

The words hung in the air like a mushroom cloud and the roar of the band cancelled out everything. A hand grenade going off backstage would not have been noticed.

It was usually at this point, thirty seconds into the first song, that whoever was in the star's dressing room would start to get *real* nervous.

Detroit bands like the MC5 never ran out of guitar picks. They had backup everything. They didn't go out with silk scarves, either. They had towels. They were going to sweat and bleed. They wanted a stranglehold on the collective throat. There were no pauses while the band decided what song to play next; one ran right into the next. They played their limit and, at the last second, knocked over their equipment, set off smoke bombs, and then dashed through the plumes to the dressing room where the girls waited with more towels and lightning-fast oral sex that helped "calm everybody down," as John would say. Meanwhile, the audience and the next band were in shock.

To the wandering British bands, Detroit was, at first, just a stopping point in the middle of nowhere, a floating rehearsal opportunity prior to the "big gig" in New York or L.A. Many British bands would drift down to the Grande totally unaware that they were walking into a trial by fire and that many times their careers in the United States hung in the balance. But it didn't take English bands long to realize the threat of Detroit bands, groups like the MC5, Bob Seger's System, the Frost, Catfish, Ted Nugent, the Stooges, Mitch Ryder.

What made Detroit bands so exciting—their heaviness, their rawness—

Howlin' Wolf
arrives at the Grande, 1969

was also what kept most of them in Midwestern obscurity. Detroit bands were so raw, in fact, that most didn't know you had to create and promote your image yourself. Not until the major labels had signed up everybody in California did they turn their attention to Detroit. First to land a contract was the MC5; they actually did have a paper promo trail, thanks to John Sinclair.

Detroit bands treated gigs like drag races. The best band would win, and somebody'd be in the audience looking for an act to discover. If that didn't happen, Detroit bands just rehearsed harder and longer. It didn't matter that the English guys from way out of town were the ones that Russ Gibb hyped for weeks on the radio. Detroit bands were only too happy to blow their shit right off the stage.

Detroit was focused on itself and didn't care what was going on in New York or San Francisco or London. In those other places, it was the hype, churned out and published worldwide, that mattered. The bands read their own hype . . . and believed it.

When the Grateful Dead played the Grande, it had all the excitement of a crowd waiting for a bus that never arrived. The Dead had specified in their contract that no other acts perform with them because "the band had

John Sinclair press conference
smoking a joint for photographer
Ann Arbor, Michigan, 1968

a tendency to play all night." They did, and what a load of bullshit. Since LSD was not yet illegal, the roadies had been handing out tabs to everyone since soundcheck. It didn't take long before the whole building was blitzed on acid; a massive, mumbling throng that had collectively forgotten what they were there for.

Eventually, the Dead wandered onstage and proceeded to play some of the sloppiest bullshit that anyone had ever heard. The acid-zombies in the crowd didn't know what was going on. Could it really be this bad? This was, after all, the Grateful Dead. What about *Time* magazine? What about the blizzard of news clippings touting how radical, cool, and hip they all were? Minus the acid, the Dead would've been booed right off the stage for their wimpy, out-of-tune, Haight-Asbury hippie folk songs that went on forever in a sea of goofy band smiles. This night, a thousand or so hardcore Detroit rock and rollers tried to adjust to being speechless. They'd shown up for a blow-out barbeque, and were served Cream of Wheat.

Eventually, Uncle Russ stopped booking the San Francisco zombie guys altogether. Acid just wasn't an appropriate drug for Detroit. Tripping on a freeway, in a factory, in a riot, or at the Grande? No way. Weed and speed, that was the Motor City way, and if you wanted to party, you threw in some whiskey.

Outside the Grande, the war, the draft, race riots, and shifty politics hung in the air like a dark fog. Inside, the fog was forgotten. Russ Gibb, pied piper of FM radio, a mysterious shaman who played their music, and spoke—even coined—their language lured the kids in. From Russ's mouth, once-derogatory terms like "freaks," "factory rats," and "hippies" became self-actualizing handles young people wore with pride.

The Grande's usual schedule was three bands a night every Friday, Saturday, and Sunday. John Lee Hooker, Fleetwood Mac, Muddy Waters, Steve Miller, Howlin' Wolf, Savoy Brown, Ike and Tina Turner. Chuck Berry's first gig after prison. Cream's first tour. There was Hendrix, the sly prophet, one foot fixed in reality, the other treading the divine. Janis Joplin, out front after the show, chugging Southern Comfort with a gaggle of teens from Pontiac. The whiz kid guitarist Joe Walsh, so good your ears would spin. Iggy Pop, crawling across the stage like your deranged nephew, with all the charm of an overturned garbage can. The MC5 rapping like a jackhammer, amped on uppers and THC capsules, begging the narcs to bust them onstage. Dave Miller, art student-turned-Grande-announcer, swigging wine, then taking the mic with his pet boa constrictor coiled round his neck. British acts like Traffic, Rod Stewart, Jeff Beck, and Procol Harum hit the Grande cold and found rock and roll heaven, people hanging on every move, every note. Moths to the flame.

The Grande was a magical place, the Ealing Club times fifty. The 1968 holiday season was no exception. We ran an ungodly seventeen shows, seventeen nights straight. Joe Cocker, Procol Harum, Fleetwood Mac, Eric Clapton, the Who, Jefferson Airplane—we were moving 'em in and moving 'em out, filling the house, then cleaning it up, boom-boom-boom, here comes another band.

Jeff Beck
at the Grande, 1969

For sheer terror, nothing matched Arthur Brown, British psychedelic freak, who showed up Christmas Eve wanting to jam after his big gig downtown. He had a hit single with "Fire," which Pete produced and played bass on, that opened with Brown's spoken-word "I am the God of Hellfire and I bring you F-I-R-E!" We should've been closing down, but, what the hell, it was Christmas Eve. Suddenly, this eerie-sounding B-3 organ kicks in with a riff that sounds good and evil at the same time, the kind of riff that'd play in your head if you realized you were just about to be stabbed. Brown strides onstage in a full-blown Druid devil outfit, wearing a horse's head mask. "I am the God of Hellfire and I bring you . . . " Mid-song, he opened up a Bible—nicked from his Holiday Inn hotel room, I'm guessing—tore out the pages, and tossed them into the overly buzzed, totally aghast crowd.

I thought for sure lightning would strike or the building would burst into flames. After all, it was the birthday of Christ.

Another night, two guys cased the place, flashing badges and scaring the hell out of anybody smoking pot, which was virtually everyone. The pair would confiscate the drugs and then order the pot-smokers to leave or charges would be pressed against them and they'd be taken to jail. I thought the two guys were narcs who were being cool about it, never hauling anybody off. Turns out they were just two clowns walking around getting free drugs. Ultimately, the phony narcs were busted and taken off to jail—by two real narcs. That was the same night that Dave Miller, the Grande announcer, had gotten way too blasted, stumbled into the stars' dressing room, and power-puked everywhere. A bunch of it had landed on Grace Slick, just minutes before she was to go on.

Then there was Led Zeppelin's first two-night stand at the Grande on their debut American tour. Russ had talked up the band on the radio, calling them the "re-formed" Yardbirds and playing old Yardbirds records that were ho-hum at best. Nevertheless, a huge crowd arrived that Friday night for the "Led Birds," underestimating everything.

The band, their 300-pound manager, and a pair of roadies had shown up for soundcheck at four that Friday afternoon. Their equipment had not. It was still back at the airport in Boston. All they had were their guitars and a bass, which they'd hand-carried on the plane.

On the stage, testing their equipment, was the opening act, a four-piece pop band, kids from the suburbs setting up for their first big gig. Their mom-and-pop management team were down on the dance floor, coaching these raw kids through a squeaky version of "Good Rockin' Tonight."

Back in my office, the catering room in the ballroom's heyday, the huge English manager was making calls and hanging up on God knows who, while the Yardbirds retreads stood around chain-smoking and looking like they were about to face a firing squad. Eventually, it was determined that the gear would never arrive in time for the show and that all the music stores in Detroit had just closed, or were about to close, and, no, they didn't know who Led Zeppelin was. Soon the manager-parents were in deep negotiations with the giant Englishman flanked by the spaced-out musicians from England. From across the dance floor, it looked like a mugging waiting to happen.

The kiddie band equipment was just that, Sears-Roebuck-type stuff. Turns out, it wasn't even paid for; they were buying it on time. The parents' first reaction to the Led Zep proposition of borrowing their gear was no; they'd heard that bands from England break up their equipment. But after about thirty minutes of haggling, the Englishman finally gave them a deal they couldn't refuse: he'd pay them 300 bucks to use the drums and amps, and would give them a $1,000 deposit against any damages, and they could hold the cash. After all, Led Zeppelin would only play for an hour, and if they couldn't use the equipment, they'd have to cancel the show and the kids would lose their one big chance to play at the Grande.

The place was packed that night. I would never have guessed it, as the only thing the Yardbirds had going for them since Clapton had left was that they were from England. The kids played about half an hour and it was almost good, just bouncy, Top 40 stuff. They were so young, the audience loved them, dancing along, smoking joints, laughing. During the break, the Zeppelin roadies went onstage and moved a couple of things, but there just wasn't much there. The vocal mics went into the house PA; Dave Miller fiddled with levels. The tiny amps and bright blue wedding-reception drums would have to do.

As the band took the stage, strapping on guitars and adjusting things, Robert Plant apologized, humbly mumbling that their equipment was still in Boston, their record wasn't out, and generally setting up the packed crowd for a certified failure. The group was visibly scared as they launched their set, which amounted to their forthcoming album. But as Plant's voice and Jimmy

Page's burning guitar filled the building, people were stunned, it was so good. No echo chambers, no wah-wah pedals. The band was on edge. They were using the same tools as the kids before them, yet everything about them was new. The look. The sound. The material. They didn't do one Yardbirds tune—and nobody even missed it.

The Grande audience emptied out into the city that night with news of the greatest band that had ever played the club—and told their friends that they were playing again the next night. Needless to say, we were double-packed for the second show and had to turn people away. The band's equipment arrived, and though they were good with all the gadgets, big amps, and their own PA, in the dozen or so times I saw Led Zeppelin over the years, they never came close to sounding or playing as good as they had that first night at the Grande.

Dan Carlisle and Dave Dixon
WABX Detroit, 1969

CHAPTER EIGHTEEN

Tommy

On the 1968 Who tour that I road-managed, Pete was always writing in his notebook or reading any of the half-dozen paperbacks he kept strewn in his bus booth, the area that was supposed to be the "kitchen" but wound up as Pete's writing suite. I doubt if he drank more than ten beers on that bus the entire tour, he was so engrossed in his work.

The rest of us gathered around the other booths, banquette seating with pop-up tabletops, and told jokes or watched Moon try to invent card tricks. Roger would read music magazines, a lot of them English and European. Pete rarely wandered back to shoot the breeze, and we rarely bothered him; we were afraid he'd lose his train of thought.

When we'd finally get to our motel, Pete would take a tape recorder and an acoustic guitar in with him and work up demos of the songs he was writing on the bus. If you walked past his room, you'd hear him playing and singing. You wouldn't want to knock and stop something that was trying to be born.

By 1969, Pete had given birth to a monumental project, the first musical work to be dubbed a "rock opera." He called it, simply, *Tommy*.

The Grande was the logical place for *Tommy*'s American premiere. The club's audience was the best the Who'd ever played for—anywhere. The acoustics alone were worth the trip, plus it was the perfect size: not bar-crowd small, not convention-center big. Packed for the Who, we could get 1,500 fans in, which was way past legal.

The only glitch: the record wasn't available in stores yet. There were a few advance copies of the album at a few FM stations, but all AM had was the "Pinball Wizard" single, which they weren't spinning much. Actually, the only station that was playing anything from *Tommy* was WKNR, Uncle Russ Gibb's show. No one had any idea what an opera from the Who might be like. Some Grande regulars were predicting fat ladies in tutus and violins. It was anyone's guess.

Pete and the guys took the stage in T-shirts, looking like the regular Who, and proceeded to play an hour of music that was both complex and uplifting.

Russ Gibb
WKNR radio studio
Detroit, 1969

James Gang
after mixing Thirds
Cleveland

After a short pause, they came back onstage and played some old familiar Who tunes, plus a Chuck Berry/Bo Diddley medley that had the packed house shaking, dancing, and yelling. By the end of the band's three-night stand, they'd broken all attendance records at the Grande. *Tommy*'s colossal importance to the Who's career was not obvious at that point, but enough cutting-edge Grande customers had proven that the music was good. The word on *Tommy* was out in the epicenter city of American rock.

We threw a wrap party after the final performance. The Grande emptied out, we swept up the huge dance floor, and brought up boxes of old roller skates from the basement. We iced down a couple of cases of beer, dimmed the lights, and the band, roadies, and Grande staff skated helter-skelter on the dance floor while Dave Miller, the club announcer, spun album cuts over the PA.

Though *Tommy* had been a success, the skating was a disaster. It was a wonder nobody got killed, what with the blinding strobe lights and dozens of collisions of zooming, buzzed-out rock rats.

Thanks to his out-of-town gigs with the James Gang, Joe Walsh, the young guitarist I'd befriended at the Grande, missed the *Tommy* shows. He did

Joe Walsh
Kent Hotel, Ohio, 1969

manage to drive in from Ohio on the first night and make it to Pete's downtown Detroit hotel room at about two in the morning.

We all drank some wine, and Pete and Joe hit it off immediately. They sat on opposite beds with acoustic guitars, I set a tape recorder on the floor between them, and they played the best music I'd ever heard. It was like John Fahey and the Rolling Stones together—steaming, burning, heart-stopping guitar duos, starting with Robert Johnson right up to off-the-cuff versions of their own most recent stuff. They were humble; Pete didn't want to be Townshend the Superstar, and Walsh, the upstart whiz kid, wasn't trying to outgun him. But it was so good I was sure God wasn't gonna let me live to tell about it. I was so excited, I couldn't move.

Eventually, I passed out, and when I woke up Joe was gone, so was the cassette, and Pete was crashed out on the bed. That impromptu jam session was the beginning of a longtime friendship between Pete and Joe based on mutual musical respect that has lasted to some degree to this day: Pete, the English aristocrat, and Joe, the goofy, all-American kid.

Pete was always astounding me like that. I remember one instance, when I'd joined the band in Florida for a couple of days. John Wolf was their road manager at the time. We didn't have long, just a day and a night to fool around, but we made the most of it. By 3 AM, Pete, John, and I were partying in a swamp, which, in Florida, really wasn't all that unusual. Pete, as usual, had his guitar with him, strumming amongst the mosquitoes. Suddenly he blurted out, "I'm looking for me / You're looking for you / We're looking in at each other / And we don't know what to do / They call me The Seeker / I've been searching low and high / I won't get to get what I'm after / 'Til the day I die."

It seemed pretty darn profound.

Then he finished the song right there, as if he was on autopilot. It was so perfect, I assumed he'd already written it. But when it was over, he set the guitar down and said, "Where did that come from?"

Rock & Roll Revival

The outdoor festival. In 1969, Woodstock, the most famous of them, affirmed for the young that they were right about a lot of things. That life could be a lot of fun if you weren't hassled for being high or naked or covered in mud. That if people were just left alone, they wouldn't go crazy and hurt each other. Woodstock seemed so earthy, so natural, with the teepees and all.

Others saw it a bit differently. Promoters took a look at Woodstock and envisioned stadiums. The government watched aerial news footage of as many people gathered on Yasgur's Farm as were then stationed in Vietnam. Woodstock was under surveillance, but hardly under control. But if they'd sent in the National Guard to arrest 300,000 people for smoking pot, it would've started a revolution. So they just let it slide on its own into the mud.

The Who played Woodstock, a short set interrupted by an outburst by Abbie Hoffman, whom Pete promptly clouted on the head with his guitar.

One rainy Monday afternoon in early 1969, months before Woodstock had even crossed the public's radar screen, Russ Gibb and John Sinclair— who claimed he was moments away from signing a big money deal with Elektra Records for the MC5—took me to the downtown fairgrounds. This was Detroit, after all, so there was a track right in the middle of the city. It'd been popular in the '50s for stock car racing on the weekends, but after a new track had opened in Dearborn in the mid-'60s, it was now used only on rare occasions by General Motors as a test track to assess pothole damage to their automobiles.

A security guy unlocked a chain link fence and we wandered around what looked like an industrial junkyard on the outskirts of hell. The one-mile oval track was bumpy and cracked. In the center, several hundred new cars sat parked, covered in an inch or two of grit. Rough wooden bench seating for 30,000 ran the length of the eastern straightaway. It looked like the end of the world, and we were the only humans left.

"Well, can we do it?" Russ asked me. "I've got it for a weekend, but I say we cram it all in one day. What do you think?"

Russ wanted to put on an outdoor concert. He was in a perfect position to do so; he had the number one FM radio show at night, and was making huge money from the Grande shows and occasional events he produced at some of the big venues downtown. Rumor was that he'd made over $30,000 profit the night he brought Jimi Hendrix and Ten Years After to Cobo Hall. He never would tell me how much exactly, but I just knew he made a lot— I mean, a *lot*—of money, boxes and bags of it he left strewn around his basement until he could find time to haul it up to his car and take it to the bank. It was mostly small bills, ones and fives, and so when he finally did load up his car, it looked like he was moving to Alaska.

Russ and I both knew that Sinclair wasn't gonna be much help, but that wasn't the point. John needed to be included. If he wasn't, he could raise a stink in his little newspaper handouts and get the MC5 followers in a pissed-off or boycotting mood.

For reasons that no one else could figure out, John Sinclair had, for the last couple of years, seen himself as some sort of mystical guru figure for the kids who went to rock concerts in Detroit. In his own mind, he was already a legend of sorts. He'd discovered pot in the late '50s, when he was searching out beatniks so he could learn how to be one. Trouble was—for John, anyway—beatniks in 1950s Detroit were as rare as seat belts. Basically, there weren't any. So he'd spent years trying to write angry poetry and get it published in student newspapers and organizing jazz get-togethers in coffeehouses and on campuses. To hear him tell it, he was transforming the city. Anybody who'd talk to him or give him pot was one of "the people"— his people, he thought. In his goofy poetry, he referred to them as "the people's people." As manager of the MC5, John kept the band in a pot-stoked state of revolutionary preparedness, drumming into their addled brains that promoters were greedheads, cops were pigs, and that pot was not pot, but rather the sacrament. The gospel according to John was that pussy, music, and drugs should all be free, and, in fact, already belonged to the people— the people's people. "All Power to the People"—but he made damned sure the MC5 got paid, and considered pot by the pound as much of a band expense as guitar strings and gasoline.

"This is great," Sinclair said, lighting a joint. "This is gonna be a killer." Russ backed away a few feet, trying to keep his schoolteacher career disassociated from John's out-in-the-open drug use. That summer, Sinclair would be sentenced to prison for nearly ten years for passing two joints to undercover narcs.

I turned to Russ. "All it has is seats. There's no stage, there's no nothing."

"We can build a stage," John wheezed, holding a huge lungful of smoke and smiling. "What about Monterey Pop? That was a racetrack."

I looked at Russ like I was trapped.

"Tom, I'll get you whatever you need," he said. "You hire the guys and tell me what we have to buy. And if it works, I'll give you a $500 bonus and a couple of weeks off after it's over."

I told him I didn't want any time off, that the Grande was gonna kick ass all summer.

MC5 basement rehearsal
Ann Arbor, 1968

"Okay," he said. "A $900 bonus, and you won't have to miss any Grande shows. You build it and run it. John's people—the people's people—will do the posters and flyers."

"What about Sun Ra?" John asked.

"I think I've got him," Russ said, "but his people haven't signed contracts."

Not Sun Ra, I thought. Fifteen random black guys with mostly horns honking out what they called New Jazz. They'd played once at the Grande. Jazz, it wasn't. More like loud, noisy stampede sounds that made you want to cover your ears and toss your cookies until they quit. For some reason, Sinclair thought these guys were something special. They were more like the interpretative stage-show of a migraine headache.

"We're gonna go to all this trouble for the MC5 and Sun Ra?" I asked, skeptical.

Peter Rivera of
Rare Earth
Dallas, 1970s

Russ laughed. "Don't worry. You'll approve of everybody else."

"Like who, for instance?" I asked.

"Not 'til you commit," Russ said. "Nobody can play without a stage."

"What about all these cars?" I protested.

"We'll cover them, build a fence or something."

"Who's playing, Russ?" I tried again.

"Are you onboard?"

I gave in. Not because I particularly wanted to do the show, I just didn't want anybody else to screw it up, especially John's "people."

"So who's on the bill?" I pressed as we headed back.

"Well, let's see," said Russ, "Seger, Nugent, Frost. . . ."

"Okay, okay, who else?"

" . . . James Gang, Dr. John, Johnny Winter, and did I say Chuck Berry?"

"Holy shit, Russ, in one day? Now we're talking. I'm gonna need some lumber."

It was a round-the-clock construction and landscape mission, pulled off in a week and a half by an amphetamine-fuelled crew of Grande staff and friends. We built the stage from existing garbage lying around the fairgrounds, brought in forty-nine dump truck loads of sand, and went through twenty-four gallons of latex paint.

The festival ran like clockwork, like the Grande al fresco, an outdoor concert of the highest octane. Because everything had been thought of and worked out ahead of time, the bands—nearly thirty of them—had a blast, the performances near-perfect.

The festival's only awkward moment was when Johnny Winter, the albino bluesman, took the stage the first night. It was Winter's first outdoor concert. Our light guy up in the bleachers hit him with two super-trooper spots. Already nervous, and now blinded by the blazing spotlights, Johnny could barely function. The crowd didn't notice; this was their first look at the mysterious Delta blues guy with the flowing snow-white hair, and here he was under the glare of autopsy lighting. We quickly sent a runner up to the bleachers to shut down the spots, and Winter cranked out a set to remember.

I honestly don't know how I survived the festival. Someone took a few pictures when it was all over. In one of them, I'm standing in front of the now-dilapidated stage shredded to bits by kids wanting a souvenir of the show, a half-empty Jack Daniels bottle in my hand. I'd just chug-a-lugged the first half. In the next picture, I'm face down in the sand. It was 4 AM and were it not for the speed residue in my system, I would've passed on right then and there. At the time, I thought Russ Gibb would send a limo so the governor could award me the Medal of Honor, along with the Purple Heart. After all, three days, thousands of kids, and twenty-nine bands later, nobody had died, or even gotten hurt.

Four Dead in Ohio

Kent, Ohio. Joe Walsh, getting over his first and stickiest divorce, moved to the small town with the big college. He rented rooms for us—himself, his crew, and me—at the Kent Hotel, a rundown student/hippie/wino hangout six blocks from the Kent State campus. Joe'd described it as a little bit of heaven, with more college chicks, keg beer, and cornfield pot than you could shake your stick at. The album, *James Gang Rides Again*, still wasn't finished, so Joe'd play guitar all day at the hotel, and then at night he and the band would drive up to Cleveland to record or play gigs in one of a zillion beer-'n'-blues joints.

Life was blissful, in an *Animal House*, porn-dorm sort of way. I spent sober moments of my day making and mailing tapes of Walsh's music to Townshend in London, cuts like "The Bomber" from the James Gang's unfinished album, while Townshend sent me tapes for Walsh, stuff like the Who's unmixed *Live at Leeds*. Pete had done a few interviews with an upstart magazine called *Rolling Stone* and mentioned that his new favorite American guitar player was a white guy from Ohio named Joe Walsh. After the interview hit the stands, the James Gang began working four or five nights a week, instead of one or two.

One afternoon, a stranger showed up unannounced at the studio and introduced himself as Little Richard's manager. Richard was suffering from terminal stomach cancer, the manager shared with us, and had very few months to live. But since he was in town, and if we could come up with some serious money, the manager thought that Little Richard was well enough to drop by and play piano on some tracks. Maybe. Little Richard making his swan song on the new James Gang album? Joe's record company reps coughed up several thousand dollars in cash on the spot.

Sure enough, Richard showed up in about an hour and hung around for two days doing overdubs and singing some old gospel tunes. We thought for sure we were seeing the very last of Little Richard. And the James Gang wasn't the only white-boy band that, as if by divine intervention, had the opportunity to have Little Richard contribute to their recordings.

Joe Walsh
Kent Hotel, Ohio
1969

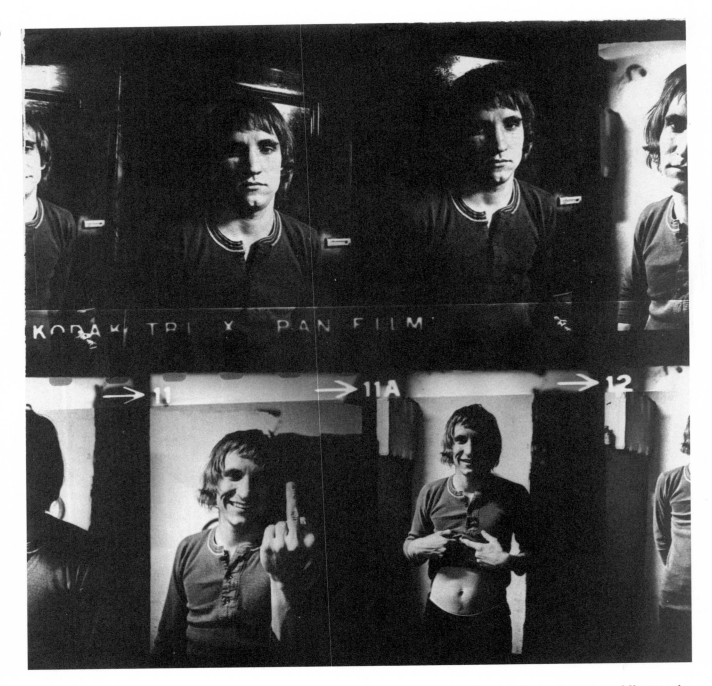

KODAK TRI X PAN FILM

→ 11 → 11A → 12

Joe Walsh

Nixon, at this time, was trying his best to throw a canoe paddle into the whirlwind of the musical renaissance. College students made the politicians nervous; just seeing Nixon on the tube or hearing his voice made us nervous. As far as telling us to go to Vietnam and get shot at—hey, wait a minute. The kids in the Midwest said he didn't have the authority. That's exactly why I moved to Detroit. I'd been all over the U.S., and every time I met somebody my age I'd ask, "How are you staying out of the service? Are you going to Canada? Student deferment?" In Detroit, the answer was always, "Fuck no. I was born here. I'm not going anywhere. If they want to fly me halfway around the world to get shot at by strangers, they can shoot me in my front yard. I won't say I'm a homosexual or in the White Panthers. I've already got my own M-16." And the draft board? Well, someone had bombed the Ann Arbor draft board in the middle of the night. Thirty-thousand names blown into confetti. Not too many went down to reregister.

Just as the James Gang album was finished, shooting broke out at the college and four students were killed. We watched in disbelief as tanks and jeeps rolled through the streets, Joe standing at the window, guitar over his shoulder, still strumming, a live soundtrack as it was all happening. Then the door was kicked in, we were swarmed by National Guard combat troops in full battle gear and gas masks, and bayonets were shoved in our faces. After they'd done a strip search of all of our rooms, the soldiers told us they'd seen Joe in the window and thought his guitar was a rifle.

The new martial law in Kent made it possible for cops and troops to sweep the hotel, rounding up all the drug dealers and underage girls. Needless to say, it made life pretty uncomfortable for the rest of us, so within days we packed everything in a van and trailer and hit the road, playing anywhere we could, holding our collective breath until the album was released. The first single, "Funk #49," was a radio smash. The gigs got bigger, the bell-bottom girls gave way to chicks in miniskirts and heels, and if we hadn't been on the move constantly we'd have spun out of control.

Timothy B. Schmidt, Joe Walsh, and Smokey Wendell
Long Run tour, Dallas, 1980

Soon I got a call from Russ Gibb. He was organizing another outdoor festival, wanted to know if the James Gang would play, and asked if I'd manage the stage. Already on the bill were Rod Stewart, Mountain, Bob Seger, Ten Years After, Joe Cocker, the MC5, and Jethro Tull. We were in.

When Gibb had seen the footage of Woodstock, he counted heads and looked at the mess. Russ had made plenty of money from the Rock & Roll

Revival, and was ready to give it another, bigger go. First on his to-do list: find himself a self-made multimillionaire.

Dick Songer, at age sixteen, had put a down payment on an old dump truck to do small-load hauling in Detroit. He paid his own bills from then on. By the time he sent himself through college, he had six trucks on the road, plus two small bulldozers, and drove a loaded white pickup that smelled new from across the street. Songer was forty-two when he met Russ Gibb, his company now responsible for building the majority of highways and bridges in Michigan. He was also one of the first guys in Detroit to own a helicopter; turbo, top of the line with jet boosters. With that helicopter, he was at every job site, every day, all over the state. He had a pilot and spent most of his time staring out the window, shopping for property.

Songer owned a parcel near Jackson, Michigan, 400 acres with a lake in the middle and three miles in circumference. He sent a crew to smooth out the rolling hills and meadows, all former grazing and farm land, and to spread the highway grass seed. Other than sending in the mowers once or twice a year, Songer was content to just fly over the place in his chopper, making sure it looked beautiful. Then Russ came along. Cha-ching!

Now with Songer as his partner, Russ had unlimited financial backing, 400 acres to fool around with, and a team of builders who could build anything fast. Russ had watched all that'd gone wrong at Woodstock: cars jamming the roadsides, people lining up for Porta Johns, folks simply walking over the fences without paying admission, the entertainment running hours behind schedule. Russ knew he and Songer could do better.

Goose Lake Festival
from the roof, Michigan, 1970

So after a bunch of meetings over blueprints, it was agreed that Songer would finance and build a permanent outdoor concert facility functional for crowds of 400,000, with paved parking for 12,000, plus hundreds of acres of marked-grass parking. Soon the on-paper plans were reality. There were permanent restrooms built throughout the grounds with abundant private showers and laundry sinks. The stage and sound towers were built from bridge steel. There were playgrounds and campgrounds, picnic areas, laundry facilities, loads of water fountains, and a chain link fence twelve feet high, built so well it could have circled the Smithsonian. Lifeguards were stationed every 100 feet on the lakeshore, and a medical tent that could handle anything was staffed with doctors and med students who'd jumped at the chance to volunteer their time. Tickets were custom-made poker chips from Vegas that were impossible to fake. When kids started showing up a week before the show, Songer bought up another 300 acres across the road

Patrick Cullie and cop
Goose Lake, 1970

from the festival entrance so the would-be gatecrashers could camp out without trespassing on others' property. It also kept gawkers and squatters from entering the site before we were ready for them.

The Goose Lake International Music Festival took place August 7, 8, and 9, 1970. Russ was still booking the bands days before the gig. Joan Baez was not asked to play, nor was Country Joe. Instead, Russ assembled a monster bill that included Savoy Brown, Jethro Tull, Joe Cocker, Ten Years After, Savage Grace, Mountain, Chicago, RAM, Bob Seger, John Sebastian, Alice Cooper, Litter, SRC, the James Gang, the Stooges, John Drake Shake, Flock 3, Power, Mighty Quick, Brownsville Station, the Flying Burrito Brothers, and Suite Charity. Alice Cooper, Joe Cocker, and Savoy Brown didn't perform—they'd never signed contracts—so the MC5 and Rod Stewart were added late.

I designed the entire five-acre performance and backstage area with Patrick Cullie, a former college student who helped me out with the James

Gang. We printed up a detailed flowchart showing how the bands would load their equipment in and out, along with handmade blueprints of the stage, dressing rooms, and groupie tent. We scheduled the band lineups for each of the three days and sent them to the newspapers, which were permitted to publish them one week before the show.

Our backstage area, off-limits to the press, was fenced and patrolled. There, we parked nine brand-new house trailers, which served as the bands' dressing rooms. A large circus tent, stocked with beer in ice tubs, also doubled as the designated groupie area, with twenty or thirty sizzlers on standby, instructed not to leave the tent unless they were invited. We had horseshoe pits and half-court basketball, and the load-in area could handle four semis at a time.

Like the Rock & Roll Revival, Goose Lake went off virtually hitch-free. My revolving stage design ensured that the band changeovers went smoothly and quickly. And it also came in handy when Iggy Pop thought he'd start another song after the Stooges had played their allotted twenty minutes. I cut his power, spun the stage, and there was Ten Years After, guitars blazing. Rod Stewart had so much fun performing Friday night that he had his road manager phone Bill Graham that he had laryngitis and had to cancel his Saturday night gig at the Fillmore, the most important rock venue in the nation. Rod spent Saturday sitting on the side of the stage, drinking wine and watching Mountain and Jethro Tull.

Though the press was given free passes, they were outraged—*Rolling Stone*, in particular—that they were not allowed backstage to mingle and took their revenge by not writing about the event. A few publications did, though, like *Billboard*, which described Goose Lake as the largest paying crowd in the history of music, with 365,000 attendees. A few thousand more had shown up at Woodstock the year before, but only 50,000 paid. And whereas at Woodstock everything was eight hours late, at Goose Lake, everything was four minutes ahead of schedule. I busted my ass.

The government, on the other hand, didn't care that the bands were great, that things ran on time, that problems were solved before they even came up, that nobody got hurt. They saw Goose Lake as a too-large-for-comfort conflagration of hippies hell-bent on smoking pot, and took it upon themselves to keep it from ever happening again. The governor slammed the whole Goose Lake facility with an injunction that closed the park until further notice. Gibb and Songer were accused of creating an outdoor drug market. And since the festival hadn't been covered in the national press, people who did hear about its demise just assumed it'd been a pile of chaos—or maybe some sort of evil plot.

Bob Seger
Detroit, 1969

The Hard Corps

The first time Rod Stewart had come to the Grande was with Jeff Beck, with Ron Wood playing bass. While everyone was there for Beck's guitar work, I was knocked out by Stewart's voice. A few months later Rod returned with the Faces, with Ron Wood playing guitar.

After the show, I told Rod that I'd taken some shots of Jeff Beck, that he was in some of them, and that there were a few lying around the office. Rod wanted to see them. What really got his attention, though, was the stuff I'd taken in Europe. He'd been to Paris many times; Ibiza, too. He came across one of my Paris street photos and got really excited. He'd just finished a solo album, *Gasoline Alley*, and thought the street shot would make the perfect album cover. He used the Grande office phone to call the record company in Chicago and tell them. It was one o'clock in the morning; Rod woke up a lot of people only to learn that the record company had already printed 100,000 album jackets featuring a watercolor painting of a manhole cover. Since he was untested as a solo artist, Rod was in no position of power, and so after an hour of calling this guy and that guy, he hung up the phone and said, "Well, we can't use it. But our flight isn't 'til three tomorrow. You should take some shots of the band in the morning before we leave. I'll get the lads ready, so just come by the hotel at ten and we'll do it." He and Ron took a cab from the Grande. I called the Hard Corps.

The Hard Corps—that's what me and my collection of guys called ourselves. The name was a take-off on Apple Records, the Marine Corps, and porn in general. The group was a ragtag assemblage of friends I'd made at the Grande, mostly roadies and musicians who could be counted on to do the impossible, to make things work simply because the guys would endeavor to the point of exhaustion—and then keep going. People who couldn't keep up were regarded as "not hard corps." Our motto: "You expect more from the Corps . . . and you get it."

Most of the Hard Corps were living in teepees at the Third Power "farm," a wooded property where the popular regional band Third Power threw their legendary parties. Other acts would venture out to the farm for photos.

Bob Seger and band
taking the oath

Once there, they'd have to do things the Hard Corps way. Like Bob Seger's band, the System. When they arrived, photo wardrobe in hand, we told them, "Hang your clothes on this tree, we're ready to administer the oath." We pulled out the Boy Scout manual, and they had to hold up their right hands and repeat after us, things like "be prepared" and "help others" and "do the right thing." There we were, a bunch of rock and roll guys out in the woods at the height of 'Nam, everybody smoking dope 'til the tops of their heads were ready to blow off, and all of a sudden we were caught up in the Boy Scout oath. It really made for a solemn moment. We felt like we'd said something profound, something important. "I pledge allegiance to God and Country. . . ." You can't go through all those words and not have them affect you.

So it became our routine, making everyone take the oath before sitting around the fire to get high with the guys. Ted Nugent came out and took the oath. He was definitely not a pot-smoker, but he took the oath just to get his picture made. The oath was all we had to hang on to. Nobody could get behind Nixon. The oath served as something. We'd start it out laughing, but by the time we finished, we were dead serious.

So at two in the morning I called out to the farm and told "Chuch" Magee, the stuttering Third Power roadie and a key Corps soldier, that we had a photo session with an English band in the morning and I needed his help.

Faces
Ann Arbor, Michigan, 1970

Chuch said he could get the limo running by dawn and would pose as a driver. He added that Patrick Cullie, who helped me with the James Gang and Goose Lake, was sitting in the kitchen rolling joints, but he could come along too, pose as a writer and interview the band.

The limo belonged to the Third Power. They'd bought it from a funeral home for 500 bucks, managed to drive it to the farm a few months before, and could never get it running again. It was pretty iffy. Remarkably, Chuch got it going in a couple of hours and hand-pumped the nearly flat tires with a bicycle pump. Then he and Patrick washed, waxed, and disinfected the inside until I got there at about 7:30 AM. They'd replaced the smell of death with the smell of Pine-Sol, Patrick said proudly, but he suggested we keep the windows down 'til we got to the Holiday Inn in Birmingham, just north of Detroit city limits.

So off we went. I had a couple of cameras, a couple of handfuls of film. Chuch wore a little cap and jacket and was gonna pretend that he was his own limo company and we'd gone all out. He packed his toolbox in the trunk and planned to keep the motor running 'til the band left town.

An hour later we were in the parking lot at the Holiday Inn. We'd made a grocery stop and loaded up on fresh fruit, cheap champagne—lots of it—and orange juice and soda, and stuck it all in ice chests that we put on the floor of the limo. We were set and speeding like you wouldn't believe. I'd

Faces
Ann Arbor, Michigan, 1970

taken two black mollies—one when Stewart left the Grande and one when I got to the Third Power farm—so I wasn't gonna sleep or eat for about twenty-four hours. I don't know what everybody else took, but the Corps had been up all night getting everything ready, and showed no sign of fading. On the ride, we decided that we should do the shoot in a park or something. Chuch kept talking about the arboretum near Ann Arbor. It would take about thirty minutes to get there, but it was beautiful. We were charged up. Hard Corps.

I went to Rod's room and knocked. A stunning girl, about eighteen or nineteen, answered the door. I'd seen her once or twice at the Grande, but had never spoken to her.

"Rod's in the bathroom," she said, "but he told me to give you this room list. He told everybody except Mac about the pictures. Mac's not answering his phone, so we don't know if he's here."

I went to Mac's room first; band photos without the full band wouldn't work. I knocked. Then I knocked some more. Then I banged like I was with the SWAT team. Eventually, the door opened a crack. I could see a nose and eye over the little brass chain.

Rod Stewart
on East and West coast time
Ann Arbor, Michigan, 1970

Teepee outside Detroit 1970

"Who the fuck are you?" Mac demanded in a raspy voice, like he was expecting me to show some kind of badge.

"I'm the photographer," I told him, "and Rod said we're gonna shoot some band pictures this morning."

The door slammed shut. Inside, Mac was yelling at full volume. *"You tell Rod to go fuck himself. . . . I didn't get in 'til a few minutes ago and I haven't been to sleep yet. . . . I'm in no shape to take pictures. . . . Go away. . . . Don't bang on my door!"*

When I returned to Rod's room, he was dressed and ready to leave. After hearing of my run-in with Mac, Rod called him and explained that they needed group pictures for L.A., that it had to be done, and that Mac could sleep on the plane. Thirty minutes later—with the limo still running and Chuch wiping off those dust spots that are so troubling when you're speeding your brains out—the band piled into the limo. The girl knew the quickest way to get to the arboretum, so we followed her car. Inside the limo, Mac saw the Styrofoam ice chests and growled, "I hope to hell you've got some Guinness in there."

We didn't.

Holiday Inn Darkroom Checklist

CHAPTER TWENTY-TWO

For me, it was the history of the moment, not the gadget part of photography, that I liked. So I kept it simple as oatmeal. No meters. No clicking timers. No flash. No case. No lens caps. I carried a black no-extras Nikon, worn around the edges, burnished brass underneath, on a worn black leather strap, the perfect length, handmade for me by Chuch. It didn't need to be adjusted, it never came off, and it never broke.

I developed in Diafine for the grain. Time and temperature didn't matter. I could time everything in the back of my mind, measuring by bars of music, sex, or the time it took to smoke a cigarette. If I was in a hurry, I could wash my film in rubbing alcohol and dry it with a blow dryer. That way, I always had pictures of the last show before anybody could change clothes, eat, or come to my room.

Then, whatever happened, happened. The pictures kept coming out of the bathtub. The band wound up as darkroom assistants trying to get high, get drunk, get laid—and still not miss anything.

My checklist for the road:

1 large changing bag, preferably custom-made from soft natural fabrics using the store-bought bag as a pattern, since the commercial bag is made with stiff polyester.

Rare Earth billboard as seen from the "Riot (Hyatt) House," Los Angeles, 1970

2 steel developing tanks—one large and one medium (six rolls) filled with film reels.

20 large wooden clothespins (in a freezer bag)

2 "church keys," a pair of scissors, a roll of gaffer's tape (not duct tape)

1 blow dryer and at least two bottles of rubbing alcohol, Diafine developer cans, small

Fixer packages (gallon size)

1 box of photo postcard paper

1 box of 100 8x10 RC paper. If you have room, take a box of 11x15 RC

3 plastic trays

1 plastic bottle of Photo-Flo, orbit and stop bath

Several boxes of photo wipes, repacked into freezer bags and sealed so they can be used as padding

Plenty of plastic negative sleeves

1 piece of 8x10 safety glass, no scratches

3 household extension cords, the thin wire kind, and plug bar

String, pushpins, and twelve plug-in bulb sockets

24 GE red bulbs (the little bitty ones, and a few twenty-five-watters)

Portable enlarger with a great lens and three new bulbs

Tape player and a small tape recorder

Red litho to make the television red, so you can stay tuned

Tom Wright
shooting Ron Wood
early '70s

CHAPTER TWENTY-THREE

Mary Ann

The Hard Corps. Photos, promotion, concert organization, management—we could do it all, our flyers said. So when Frijid Pink needed a road crew for a two-week East Coast tour in 1970, we got the call.

Chuch, Patrick, Russ Schlagbaum (like Chuch, another Third Power roadie), Mark Patterson (ex-Grande staff who'd worked for Joe Walsh), and I piled into a van and headed to Tampa, Florida, where the band would meet us. We arrived a week early, checked into the Clearwater Hilton, and launched a plan of action. Patrick would write and place glowing press releases, we'd plaster the whole damn town with flyers and posters, and with a guerilla marketing approach we'd build enthusiasm for the shows.

The girl at the front desk was stunning. This was no rock chick. High heels, makeup, knockout perfume. I was dumbstruck. She didn't seem to take much notice of me, though. As she assembled our rooms list, I scrambled for something to say. Glancing out the glass doors of the lobby, I noticed letters going up on the marquee at the Clearwater Auditorium a half-mile away.

"Wow, Derek and the Dominoes," I tried.

"What are Derek and the Dominoes?" she said absently as she scribbled and stapled.

So much for weaseling my rock résumé. "Layla" had to be the biggest song on earth at that time and I'd found the one person on the planet who didn't know or care anything about it.

It was like someone had turned on the lights.

This girl, she was it. She was so together and didn't care a thing about music, the music that I felt was starting to control my life. Clapton meant absolutely nothing to her.

I began to reinvent myself on the spot.

"That chick with the hillbilly hairdo?" Patrick said after I told him the hotel manager had never heard of Derek and the Dominoes. "Somebody better check her pulse." Of course, Chuch had already scored Dominoes tickets for all of the Corps.

Tom Wright and son Tim
photo by Mary Ann
1972

I must've made ten trips a day to the front desk. I was obsessed.

On the third day, Mary Ann invited me to her place after work. She drove me in her car, a brand-new pale green Ford Mustang with less than 5,000 miles on the odometer. I'd never been in one. She shared a tiny house with a blonde waitress who had heard of Derek and the Dominoes, but didn't like them. When the waitress went to work, our lives changed forever.

Mary Ann and I left in her car that night. She was in a nightgown, I was in jeans and a T-shirt. We drove and talked until the sun came up. She never went back to the hotel, and neither did I.

Mary Ann was the biggest event of my life. I knew it immediately. With her, I saw God everywhere. I had never understood spiritual thought. Acid and pot opened a door that had always been there, but now I was inside. I felt so lucky to be part of it, to surrender to it. Because when you see God, you can't even consider that you're smart enough to fool the universe.

Back at her house at sunrise, Mary Ann ran in to get some clothes. Then we headed north.

Things were getting giddy and weird. Neither of us had been to sleep, she hadn't gone to work, and my guys knew nothing. We were both leaving our lives behind. She'd worked for years to get where she was, the general manager of the Clearwater Hilton, at age twenty-two. And I was . . . well, I couldn't remember. I just knew that I wasn't one anymore.

We had breakfast on the road somewhere and then spent the afternoon walking through the tiny Greek fishing village of Tarpon Springs, watching the shrimp and sponge boats return to the docks.

Back on Highway 19, we saw a hippie kid hitchhiking north. "How far are you going?" he asked as I pulled over. Before we could answer, he said he was headed to Atlanta, but that any little bit helped.

"Will you be our witness?" I blurted out.

"Sure," he said. "If you'll give me a ride, I'll be your judge and jury."

Mary Ann let him into the backseat.

Twenty miles up the road, I turned off the highway. Ten minutes later we came to a small inlet bay with a beach about a block long. No one was there. There weren't even footprints in the sand.

"What's happening, man?" the kid asked.

"It's cool," I said. "We're just gonna watch the sunset."

The kid pulled his bag from the backseat, walked away from the car 'til he had a clear view of the sun sinking low over the Gulf, sat down, and lit a joint.

I took Mary Ann's hand and we walked toward the water. We were both barefoot. When we got to the edge, I scooped her up in my arms and walked toward the sun. The water was up to my waist, but I kept going.

"Now what?" she asked in a whisper when I'd walked out as far as I could.

"Will you marry me?" I asked.

She didn't say a word.

Still holding her, I turned around to face the kid. He waved and flicked the joint off into the sand.

"I asked her to marry me!" I yelled at him.

"What did she say?" he yelled back.

"Nothing!" I screamed.

"Ask her again!" he yelled.

Mary Ann interrupted. "Wait a minute. What if I say no?"

I turned back toward the sunset. "Then I'm dropping you right here, and you can go do whatever you need to."

"I've already lost my job," she said.

I looked deep into her eyes. I'd never been so serious. I asked again. "Will you marry me?"

"Yes," she whispered.

I turned back around to face the kid on the beach.

"She said yes!" I yelled.

If he hollered back, I didn't hear it. Mary Ann cupped her hands to her mouth like a football coach shouting to the team and shouted, "*Yes!*"

The kid put his hand to his ear like he couldn't hear a thing.

And then came the scream I'll remember forever. It came from deep-down, soul-deep, and could've been heard ten blocks away if anybody but the witness were around.

"*Yeeeesss!*"

Her dainty jugular vein bulged from her neck as she screamed. I kissed it, and walked her back to the beach.

I was in a dream with a woman on the same spiritual trip. When we looked at each other, all we saw was a young boy's face—and we knew it was our son. He'd chosen us. We were from different worlds, things fell together, and now we were so far out of control, we just gave up. There was a boy on the way before we even knew he was on the way, and, ready or not, he'd chosen his parents. Who were we to go against something so strong? We were powerless to resist.

At the Dade City exit, the hippie kid got out and wished us luck. I drove on to my uncle's house. He owned a lot of land in the area, but I hadn't seen him in ten years. It was dark when we pulled into his driveway.

"Tom, what on earth are you doing here?" he asked as we hugged on his front doorstep.

"I just got married," I told him. "Do you remember when you said that, if I ever needed it, you'd give me some land? Well, how about a lot on the river?"

My uncle was visibly stunned, but he showed me a map and pointed out some property.

"Any lot you want," he said. "Do you need anything?"

"Yeah, she's wet," I said. "Can we have a blanket?"

He rummaged up some blankets and candles.

"Can we at least meet her?" he asked.

I told him Mary Ann didn't want to see anybody now and that we needed to sleep. This, I'm sure, was the strangest thing that had ever happened at my uncle's house. But he was cool.

I drove the Mustang along the deserted sand road until I realized we were near the river. I parked the car. We slept out in the open. After all, it was God's idea.

In the morning, I walked Mary Ann to the river and we swam until we felt clean. From my bag, I pulled a pair of scissors that I used to cut film. As she sat on the riverbank, I trimmed her hair, and in seconds she went from Dolly Parton curls to a Rod Stewart thatch. We swam some more. She looked extraordinary, naked, with short, clean hair. Profoundly beautiful.

I built a small hut out of palm fronds, and Mary Ann made a fire. We were both naked. She washed our clothes in the river and we hung them on trees to dry.

We stayed in the Florida woods for four or five days. My uncle came out and brought us camping cookware and a machete. He was happily baffled by the whole situation. It was all raw land, no people anywhere. We were living like aborigines—until the van showed up.

The Hard Corps. They'd reached my mom by phone; she'd heard from my uncle and told Patrick where I was. They came to the campsite with beer and pot and sleeping bags and all my stuff in the van. Bye-bye, Garden of Eden.

When they saw Mary Ann with short hair, no makeup, and a tan, they fell for her, too. They told us that the Frijid Pink dates had gone fine without me, and raved about the Derek and the Dominoes show. There were a few more Pink gigs in the Carolinas, but then it would be back to Michigan. I told them I didn't know what I was gonna do, now that I was married.

Married? They freaked out. I told them our story; they just stared at the fire. Not long before, I'd talked all of these guys out of whatever life paths they'd been journeying down to join the Hard Corps. Now I was leaving them high and dry. Life as we all knew it had come to an end.

We hatched a plan to meet back in Detroit when I came to my senses. Two weeks later, Mary Ann and I rolled into the driveway of the Hard Corps house, a place the guys and I'd rented just before leaving on the Pink tour.

It was doomed to failure before we even walked through the door.

When we'd crawled out of the palm hut by the river in Florida and returned to Michigan, I'd gone down to the courthouse and gotten a marriage license. A couple of weeks later we all—Mary Ann and I, and the Hard Corps—climbed into the van and rode around until we found a church. The guy raking leaves out front told us he was the pastor. I introduced Mary Ann, and asked him if he would marry us. "Sure," he said, "all you need is a license." Patrick, whose official Corps title was Keeper of the Stash, reached into his leather shoulder briefcase and handed me the document. I gave it to the preacher.

"When were you thinking to have the wedding?" he asked.

"How about right now?" I answered.

"Well," he said, shaking his head, "I really need to bag these leaves. And I'd need to change."

"We'll get the leaves," Chuch piped up.

CHAPTER TWENTY-FIVE

Senior Citizens Alert

From: Tom Wright
Sent: Mon, 17 Jul 2006
To: Pete Townshend
Subject: senior citizens alert

Hi Pete,

If I don't go down in flames, I will land in Frankfurt on the 19th and goose-step to the Alps to see you on the 20th. The buzz in the U.S. is that the trimmed-down version of the show is turning into a must-see event. I, for one, am looking forward to it.

Cheers, Tom

From: Pete Townshend
Sent: Monday, July 17, 2006
To: Tom Wright
Subject: Re: senior citizens alert

Can't wait to see you again. Have a safe journey. Pete

Pete Townshend
Houston, 1982

The Paleo Festival in Nyon is, hands-down, Switzerland's best-kept secret. My friend Chris Easter and I were there to catch the new "Who's Left" tour. The festival grounds are possibly the most beautiful in the world, rolling fields surrounded on all sides by snow-capped Alps, plus a view of Lake Geneva.

A small stream sliced through a thick wood, separating the backstage area from the public grounds. To get from where the bands congregated to the stage, you had to stroll though the forest—Sherwood Forest, I kept thinking—and over a few wooden bridges. Behind the huge stage, there was a cozy lounge area complete with outdoor cafés, bars, restrooms, and washers and dryers. It was like the back garden of some college frat house, only with more women in tank tops. European women, no less. Only when you climbed the long flight of stairs and the ramp to the stage could you see that there were over 100,000 people there, ages five to eighty-five. This was truly a family affair.

During the day, Chris and I wandered all though the grounds, checking out the large, matching tents that housed food, T-shirts, and CD vendors; masseuses; and Internet cafés. Some outdoor sculpture was spread around, and at the top of a hill, a five-acre circle was planted with tall sunflowers. The restrooms, plentiful and spacious, were appointed with beautiful tile, mirrors, flower arrangements—more hotel lobby than outdoor music festival. We were amazed to find that even though there were people everywhere, there was no trash on the ground, none of the yelling or screaming or crowd noise that you'd expect. It was the third of the Paleo Festival's six days, but the atmosphere was more like a day in the park with the family, which was a good thing. There were the occasional weird hairdos and Mardi Gras getups, but, for the most part, this was civilized.

The drinking policy was BYOB, apparently, so a lot of guys were walking in with a case of beer in each hand looking for a place to settle. The whole scene was dreamlike. It really didn't matter who was going to play; these people were here just to be here. The temperature never rose past 78, and it was comfortable everywhere. Over the scent of fresh summer flowers and cedar chips on the pathways, wafted the sweet odor of hash, one of my favorites, for sure. Here, it smelled so . . . healthy. I don't think anyone was smoking pot. If they were, it would've seemed downright rude; mixed in with the hash, it would've smelled like burning garbage.

I was happily surprised to see Russ Schlagbaum, former Hard Corpsman whom I hadn't seen in years, traveling with the Who, responsible for the TV studio trailer hitched to a huge Ford diesel pickup. Since his last Stones tour in 2002, he'd refused to go out with anyone but Jimmy Buffett. He turned everybody down—until the "Who's Left" tour. "The Airstream is not meant for this kind of punishment," he now protested several times a day, "these things are meant to be driven to Florida once a year and parked."

Townshend had had that Airstream for years, juiced with enough power to broadcast live on the Internet from backstage at every show. Now it's a forum for Pete's girlfriend Rachel, who sings like an angel and talks Cockney when she's relaxed. She's beautiful and Pete adores her; the TV thing is his

Roger Daltrey
Los Angeles, 1968

way of showing it. Rachel's the hostess of In the Attic, a daily production with her songwriting friend Mikey. Pete sits quietly behind them, accompanying Mikey's new tunes on acoustic guitar. I couldn't watch much of it; it was a new chemistry, seeing Pete humbling himself to someone as inexperienced as Mikey. "When are people on this tour gonna start treating me like a star!" Mikey often says to no one in particular, while he's hanging out backstage waiting for others to get set up for the day. I hoped he was kidding, but I couldn't tell.

It's this sort of talk that drives Russ up the wall. "Six months ago, this guy was living on the dole in his mother's basement, and now he's on salary of ten grand a month writing songs for Rachel and doing this TV thing," Russ mutters while he hooks up the air-conditioner to the outside of the trailer to make it bearable inside with all the lights and stuff.

Pete and Rachel had flown in from Pete's villa in France and arrived at the festival at about 5 PM. By then, the Airstream studio was up and running and Pete's dressing room bus was nice and cool.

"I see you made it safely," Pete said to me, as he stepped off the bus and headed for the studio. I hadn't seen him since our tea at Eel Pie three months earlier; his tone was like we hadn't seen each other since lunch.

We stopped at the entrance to the broadcast trailer. Pete had a Gibson twelve-string in his left hand and a Collins guitar in his right.

"Wow," I said. "Do you play that Collins onstage? Those are made in Austin by some really cool people."

Pete set the twelve-string down and leaned it against the Airstream. He held the Collins up to me like it was a tray of champagne.

"These," said Pete, "are the finest guitars on the planet Earth. I bought this one used in New York three years ago. I paid $15,000 for it, and I think I have played it every day since. I don't play it onstage because I don't want anything to happen to it. Besides, I have an arrangement with Gibson guitars, so playing someone else's acoustic onstage wouldn't exactly be fair."

He picked the twelve-string back up. "It's good to see you," he said. "We'll talk later. We're getting ready to do this Internet show. You can watch here."

He pointed to a large video monitor set up in front of what looked like Mikey's mom's patio furniture under the Airstream's awning.

Instead, I wandered off and found Chris in the catering area, a restaurant for bands and crew under a circus tent, complete with chefs behind the counter and a wall of glass-doored coolers stocked with every kind of beer known to man, Italian sparkling water, yogurt, fruit, you name it. If you wanted steak or sushi, you'd ask one of the chefs; otherwise there was the standard buffet of cheeses, breads, sliced roast beef, trays of rice and vegetables, and tons of salads. We nibbled for an hour and drained a couple of frosty Heinekens.

Way after dark and about an hour before the show, I ran into Roger in the artists' lounge area. I could tell I was the last guy he expected to bump into in Switzerland. He was his usual preshow jittery self, as if he wanted to vacuum up the vibe and get a handle on how the audience was gonna treat the Who. As if there was any question. It was obvious to me that the 100,000 or so people sitting out in front of the stage were looking forward to the Who. They were the headliners after all.

But Roger seemed edgy, and now that he had an American to vent to he proceeded to address me like I was George W. Bush's personal advisor, giving me the BBC/CNN take on the war in Iraq. Everything bad in the world was Bush's fault. "Don't be stupid, Roger," I said. "Bush is the American Churchill." "Bullshit," he said. "It's all about oil. . . ." and so on and so forth. After a while, his assistant brought him a note and they wandered off toward the production office. I set off to find Chris since the show was about to start.

When I found him, I double-checked that he still had the all-access pass that Russ had loaned him that afternoon. It was an extra and sure made things easy. It also meant that during the show we'd be on the stage, off to the side. I got Chris situated at stage right, where he had a great view of the band just ten feet from the bassist. I headed to stage left, closer to Pete, in Alan Rogan and Bob Pridden territory. I couldn't see the bass player, but it was no matter; I wouldn't have known this guy if I'd have bumped into him.

Like any Who show, it was hard to take my eyes off of Townshend. I watched him fiddle with the amp knobs, grab picks, yell at Rogan to adjust the stage monitor speakers, or change and tune guitars in the middle of a song. With Pete, everything's always happening at once, and it's all exciting to watch.

After two or three songs, I wandered out in the crowd and stood at what would have been the fifty-yard line, what Dale Peters of the James Gang calls "the sweet sound spot." Live music always sounds good onstage, but out in the crowd, that's the product, that's what everyone pays their ticket money to hear. Out there, the sound is totally different. And it used to be a crap shoot. The Stones once had this goofy sound guy who was drunk and coked up all the time, and going deaf. For ten years the Stones had no idea how bad they sounded live; they never stood in the audience. After the "Bridges to Babylon" tour, the crappy sound guy got the boot. Ever since, with their new man mixing out front, they've never gotten a bad sound review.

Watching the Who ignite in a Swiss meadow, I felt good for the band. They sounded great. Zak Starkey, never much of a heavy hitter, had finally gotten the message and was now playing with fire, covered in sweat by the second song and breaking as many sticks as Moon used to. The band, in all of its sweat-soaked glory, was broadcast around the venue on video screens so tall I could count Pete's eyelashes—hell, they were ten feet long.

I headed back onstage as they launched "My Generation," the show-closer. The band was going full-blast, and the spotlights beamed across the faces of the thousands of fans, now on their feet and shouting accolades in a half-dozen languages.

That night after the show, Russ invited Chris and me to ride along with him to Austria, through the Alps, in the dark; a twelve-hour drive, he told us. "Or," he said, "you guys can take my room. It's a beautiful hotel, only five minutes from here, and tomorrow you can take the train." This sounded better, safer, and lazier. We took him up on his offer, got a Swiss guy with the festival to call and make arrangements, and then rang for a cab.

Chit-chatting with the festival guy, I mentioned that I'd been to a lot of them, had even organized a few, and that this was the most beautiful outdoor music event I'd ever experienced.

"Yeah, it's like this every year," he said.

"Every year?" I asked, stunned.

"Yes, we've been doing this for thirty-one years," he explained. "Everybody works for free, all volunteers. If there's any money left over, we just improve the facilities and hire more bands for next year."

The next morning we set out for Austria and the Who's next gig at the Lovely Days Festival. There were a few stragglers from Paleo at the station.

We were headed to Zurich first and eventually found the right platform. As we settled in for a twenty-minute wait, I noticed an old guy nearby talking to a woman. He looked to be in his mid-seventies and could've passed for a maintenance man at the shuffleboard courts in Sarasota with his Hawaiian shirt and CIA baseball cap. The two were speaking American English, and I could hear that she was talking about her daughter who didn't want to go back to college. The guy just seemed to listen in a grandfatherly way. He was short, skinny, and appeared to be shrinking. A small bag sat on the ground next to him, a beat-up guitar case next to it. I could just make out some writing on the case, silver paint that had gone bark color, J-O-E M-C-D-O-N-. His bag covered the rest. After about five minutes, the woman left. I was intrigued by this old guy; I couldn't figure him out. He wasn't a street singer—too nice, too organized. Reaching for something in his bag, he moved it enough that I could finally read his full name. JOE MCDONALD. No.

I walked over with all the bravado strangers have on lonely train platforms and asked if he'd gone to the festival.

"Yeah," he said, "I played there yesterday. I'm Joe McDonald . . . from Country Joe and the Fish."

I couldn't believe it. "Would you mind if I took a picture?" I asked. "I remember you from Woodstock." I never went to Woodstock, but I did see the movie.

"Where are you headed?" I asked after I snapped a photo, trying to get the guitar case in the shot.

"I'm on tour," he said. "I'm going to Croatia, playing a jazz club there."

Our train whooshed in. Chris and I leapt on and left the little gray man standing on the platform.

"Who the fuck was that?" Chris asked. "He looked burnt to a crisp."

"Country Joe McDonald," I said, shaking my head.

Gimme an F. . . .

Bob Pridden and Pete Townshend
at Eel Pie Studio, London, 1983

Black-and-White Trade

If you don't use a digital and don't want to mess with searching for black-and-white film, you can buy color print film in the hotel lobby and get your prints in one hour. But regardless of what you do with them—pass them around or glue them into a scrapbook—more than likely they'll end up in a drawer where they'll turn purple and quietly fade away.

The history of the moment is gone.

Black-and-white film, on the other hand, is permanent, or can be if it's done right. The results, classical. The pursuit, expensive. The payback, shaky.

With black-and-white, you feel good if you get one good shot on a roll. A good black-and-white photograph is a visual poem. If it's really good, it has memorable depth. If it's great, it has visual depth and an element of humor—not slapstick humor, but a low level that's almost undetectable.

It's difficult to capture the temporary and the permanent in one moment, and so it's a big deal if you get everything you can see into one shot.

If you wait for something to happen, you'll miss it, so you anticipate about ten seconds into the future and develop your own rhythm in the very act of taking pictures.

After people know you are aware and sensitive to the situation, when they realize nothing will be spiritually jolted, they understand a lot about who you are and what you're doing.

They realize the act of taking a picture is no more alarming than wiping your forehead.

Taking a picture is participating in the moment, at the right second, when everything that's happening falls into place. Bodies blend with the architecture, expressions reflect the moment, the light balances just right, and without breaking the rhythm of the room, you nail the shot with your silent but deadly snap.

You can't wait to see the negatives.

Rod Stewart
Montreal, 1975

CHAPTER TWENTY-SEVEN

San Antonio

After I fled the French egg farm and met my son, I wandered through San Antonio, my family's new hometown. They'd moved there so Mom, with her bronchitis, could breathe.

I was instantly drawn to a group of run-down, old buildings on the river, across the street from my sister's new health food restaurant. Their architecture seemed the same as the castle I'd just left in France. The windows were all boarded up, and the place had obviously been empty for decades. A kindred hippie-spirit/student type was sweeping the sidewalk and told me that the buildings used to be a Catholic girls' school, closed now since World War II. The city wanted to tear the place down for a parking lot, but the hippie and a few others were fighting it and wanted to make an art school there.

I'd stumbled onto a custom-made situation: a young guy with a broom who was willing to work for free, a group of dusty old French-architecture-type buildings begging for restoration, and an art school that was pretty much a pipe dream and the basis of a cause that put the young and well-intentioned up against the bulldozers. I was in.

The next day I carried a stack of photos I'd printed in France back to the wannabe art school—in-your-face rock pictures, reams of European artists and street scenes from close to a decade in Europe, front-line documentation of the British Invasion. I offered to teach a photography class, if anyone was interested. Within days, I'd moved in, set up a portable darkroom, and was waiting for students. A poster I designed to advertise my rock and roll photography classes featured one of my pictures of Rod Stewart, and suddenly I had paying students who brought their own beer. They placed newspaper ads requesting old cameras or enlargers, and equipment started showing up by the pickup-truckload. I turned the students into photographers—and construction workers. Soon the old nuns' bathhouse was converted into a full-blown lab, prints washed down in the claw-footed tubs, and heretofore neglected, forgotten space was restored for art studios.

The Unknown Alcoholic
at rehab bunkhouse
Austin, Texas, 1982

Within a year, over a hundred students were enrolled in the photography classes, and the school was offering instruction in stained glass, pottery, furniture design, painting, weaving, and jewelry-making. It was our own little Ealing, San Antonio—style.

For Mary Ann, baby Tim, and myself, I found a farmhouse I could rent for eighty-five dollars a month and try to be a family man . . . sort of. This was dirt-farmer digs, the very environment in which Mary Ann was raised in rural Arkansas, a situation so awful that at age sixteen she ran away to Memphis. There, she landed a job at the Holiday Inn corporate office and got in the habit of overdressing to appear grown-up. It worked, and six years later she was in Florida running the Hilton where we'd met. For Mary Ann, a return to the dirt farm was a giant step backward.

Soon I was awarded a National Endowment artist-in-residence grant. I took it literally, and moved us into the space I was going to refurbish at the crumbly old school. Another disaster. We were on the second floor, with construction and renovation going on around us all the time. It was stressful for Mary Ann, dangerous for our son, and another sort of offbeat lifestyle that Mary Ann may have understood, but was definitely not looking for. About the time Tim started taking his first steps through the plaster dust and piles of rusty nails, Mary Ann took off for Florida with our baby. For the next sixteen years, it was daily heartbreak with midnight calls and a million trips to Florida for birthdays, Christmases, and summer vacations.

I was attempting the impossible, trying to glue a shattered mirror back together.

Southwest Craft Center
San Antonio, Texas, 1972

When thirty-year-old potter and ex-paratrooper Steve Humphrey arrived at the school in a U-Haul packed to the gills with pottery wheels and a speaker system reminiscent of the Who's early PA, I knew I'd met my new partner in crime. We combined my collection of live music tapes with his industrial-strength sound system until the school rocked like a cross between Woodstock and Army Jump School. Even the sandblaster couldn't drown out the Stones.

With his long blond hair, Humphrey looked a lot like Johnny Winter. It seemed only natural to turn Steve's artistic ability into a spectator phenomenon. We tried it out first on a group of fourth-graders, scheduled for a show-and-tell day. I moved all the power tools out of the wood shop and built a large stage at one end, painted flat black, of course. Center stage was a potter's wheel and a stool; on each side were Steve's monster speakers hooked up to a muscle-bound amp. Ten-pound cones of potter's clay waited on low tables next to the wheel. The rest of the room was empty and as clean as your grandmother's living room. A huge antique rug covered the Spanish tile floor in front of the stage, and a Tiffany-replica chandelier on loan from the stained glass teacher hung just above the wheel.

To the strains of "Sgt. Pepper's Lonely Hearts Club Band," the kids scrambled wide-eyed into this mysterious room, took their seats on the rug, and watched Steve make his entrance, white hair flowing over tanned, muscular arms. I'd bet Steve a case of beer he couldn't throw a pot in the course of one rock song, so I dropped the needle on Journey's "Wheel in the Sky," Humphrey grabbed a clay pyramid, slammed it down on the wheel, and went to work. By song's end, he'd crafted a gorgeous sixteen-inch vase. The kids were speechless. Then forty fourth-graders were on their feet, clapping and screaming. Steve was a rock star.

Word spread, and within a couple of weeks there were as many pottery students as photography students at the Southwest School of Art and Craft— and we now had two artists-in-residence.

When musician friends of mine were in town, I'd bring them to Southwest. Guys like Rod Stewart and John Hammond would stay until the wee hours, playing and singing off the balcony to the ragtag students who continued to keep the photography and pottery departments awash in beer and donated equipment. I even took Humphrey on a portion of a Who tour, passing him off as a roadie in Houston, Dallas, and New Orleans.

CHAPTER TWENTY-EIGHT

Mexico

Mary Ann and Tim were gone, but I needed to finish out my year at Southwest to keep the grant money coming in. The school had taken off like a rocket. Most classes were held at night; adults learning pottery, kiln building, painting, drawing, jewelry-making, weaving, furniture-building, and sculpture. One of the most popular departments, besides photography, was stained glass. "Yeah," said the stained glass guy one day, "you got the most students, but I've got the prettiest." That got my attention.

He wasn't kidding. There was a ton of women piecing together those bits of colored glass: divorcees, desperate housewives, college chicks, high school girls. While my students were hard at work on their assignments, I'd wander out onto the balcony shared by all the second-floor studios and sneak a peek into the stained glass room. Wall to wall women—and one girl stood out like a diamond in a sandbox.

A week after the first sighting, we bumped into each other out on the balcony. She was smoking what looked like her first cigarette. Her name was Karen, she was eighteen, and she was breathtaking. She was one of those people who was so beautiful that you simply couldn't take your eyes off of her. Golden skin, long blue-black hair, big brown eyes flecked with yellow and green when you got up close—she almost didn't look real. And in a town filled with cowboys and Mexicans, her New York accent and razor-sharp sarcasm defied reality, too.

Her sister had signed up for a jewelry class, Karen told me. It sounded like fun so she'd tagged along and wound up in the glass course. She was gonna make a Tiffany lamp for her parents' twenty-fifth anniversary. Karen's mother was Mexican, her father Irish, retired NYPD, who'd recently moved his family from Manhattan to San Antonio. I quickly made it my mission to monopolize her attention.

"My sister said you're married," Karen protested. "Separated," I corrected. It took a week or two, but soon we were going steady, in an art school fashion. She brushed off the overtures of guys on campus, I toned down my

Tom Wright

sepia-toning picture of
Ronnie Lane smoking a hash
pipe on Faces tour plane

flirtations with pretty students. Soon, I was taking her home after class, and not long after that she was staying at my place on the weekends. If I wasn't teaching, we were together. Even though I was ten years older than she was, her father seemed happy that we were together and that she was dating an artist and not some idiot cowboy in a ten-gallon Stetson.

Karen liked my photographs—not so much the rock shots, but the moody stuff from Europe. The craft center was her first hands-on experience with art, though she'd visited museums and galleries in New York. And the gorgeousness ran in the family. Her mother was a knockout, her sister too; even her younger brother was beautiful. When you passed any one of them

Karen
1974

on the street, you'd do a double take. It was an uncontrollable reaction.

One day, Pete Cortez, founder of San Antonio's famed Mi Tierra restaurant, stopped by to discuss the catering of a wedding that was to be held on the school grounds. In 1940, Pete and his wife opened Mi Tierra with two tables out on the sidewalk in front of an old coffee mill, near the farmer's market. Pete cooked, and so did his wife when she wasn't waitressing. By 1972, the restaurant was, hands down, the biggest and best Tex-Mex eatery in San Antonio and had grown to seat 700. Over the years, the Cortez family had bought most all the buildings in the Market Square area and employed nearly a thousand workers, not one a gringo. The sign that hung over Mi Tierra's door since 1944, when the Cortezes took over the coffee factory, read simply, "We Never Close."

When he dropped by the school that day, Mr. Cortez couldn't help but notice our restoration work. A student dressed in what looked like a space suit was using a Volkswagen-sized sandblaster to strip decades of loose plaster and paint from the clock-tower building. Other students and I fed sand into the machine's hopper a hundred pounds at a time. As Pete and I chatted, he mentioned that he owned a few old buildings downtown that he wanted to renovate. He invited me come down to the restaurant the next morning and take a look.

Karen and I showed up for breakfast the next day and toured several of the buildings. Built in the 1920s, they were all two stories, with that New Orleans/French Quarter look, but with cypress balconies instead of iron. And with less than fifty years' worth of paint on them, the wood was pristine. I could make it work, and offered to draw up a proposal for the job.

About an hour into the tour, Pete's son Jorge, "George," joined us. Pete explained to him the work I'd be doing and then looked at his watch and excused himself. George, Karen, and I eventually drifted back to the restaurant.

Not surprisingly, George was fascinated with Karen. He was blown away by her big-city accent and dumbstruck that she didn't speak Spanish. George seemed young and so interested and eager about everything; later, I learned he was actually only a year older than I was.

Over the next several weeks, George and I became friends. George had worked in the restaurant his entire life, I learned, and had just joined the Air Force and would be leaving soon for boot camp. One night, I invited him over to the craft center, and, as things would happen, we wound up drinking ice-cold cervezas out in the courtyard until after midnight.

Lolling under the stars, George told me the story of his father, who'd been raised by an aunt in Guadalajara. At sixteen, he hopped a train for the border, jumped off, and swam the Rio Grande. He hopped another train for San Antonio, but it was moving so fast he fell and broke his arm. Injured and untreated, George's father hopped the next train bound for the city. His arm never healed, and remained permanently disfigured.

George told me about how every member of his family worked in the business, long days, without vacations, because holidays and fiestas meant the restaurant would be twice as busy.

I told George about my first stepfather and our life in the Air Force, and my travels around Europe. When I got to the part about Spain, he hung on every word. His eyes glazed over at my rock stories. He'd heard of the Beatles and the Stones, but not the Who or Faces, and at one point, he accused me of making up group names.

So there we were, George talking in halting English, switching to Spanish—well, Tex-Mex, actually—whenever he needed to emphasize something, and me running out of steam as I realized that Jagger's lips, Pete's busted guitars, and Rod's feather boas were of no interest to my new friend. I was the first gringo George had ever spoken with, he'd tell me later. I'd never even seen a Mexican until I came to San Antonio. In fact, all I knew of their music was "Wooly Bully." Sure, Karen looked like a Mexican princess, but she knew less about the culture than I did.

Despite our differences, this was the foundation of a lifelong friendship, and soon I felt more at home at a table at Mi Tierra than I did with my own family.

George wanted me to see the real Mexico, the heart and soul of his homeland, and insisted on taking me on a six-week journey through the back roads of his country. It was like going back in time. In one small mountain town, the water supply for the whole village came from falls rushing over the ridge, caught in an aqueduct built by the French several hundred years ago to irrigate the sugar cane fields in the valley. These villagers had nothing—no TVs, no telephones. They survived with just the basics. Only the priest owned a car, a beat-up old VW. The bus bringing passengers and mail came once a day, and occasionally someone in a tiny pickup would bring in supplies.

Early one morning, George and I watched the village come to life. As the sun streamed over the mountaintop, laughing children dressed in crisp uniforms streamed down the cobblestone main street on their way to school. In the shadow of the whitewashed church with its soaring bell tower, men headed to the fields, joking with one another. Women called out happily as they tended to household chores. No one jumped into machines and sped off for the concrete city. There was no bang of garbage trucks, no squealing brakes, no roar of diesel semis hurtling down the highway. No stress, no clamor. Only smiles—worlds away from 6 AM San Antonio.

The serenity, the benevolence of it all, set George and me to thinking: did these dirt-poor people know something the more "civilized" world didn't? Does waking up in the splendor of a mountain sunrise to send your kids skipping and giggling out the front door to school, does that environment lead to spiritual peace? Had we just witnessed the secret to true happiness?

And the colors. This tiny village could have been the inspiration for the glorious Mexican wall murals that were painted on everything from garages to nightclubs back in San Antonio. Raw, primitive, and with a profusion of eye-popping greens, blues, oranges, and yellows—the village itself was a painting. I had left San Antonio with two Nikons and fifty rolls of black-and-white film. I'd always shot in black-and-white. We hadn't been in Mexico one day when I realized I'd made a terrible mistake. This whole country was color, pouring out in sunsets, oozing from the leaves in jungles and private gardens. Animals, especially chickens, were everywhere, walking bundles of blazing color, living connections to the earth.

I've shot mostly in color ever since. Even when I use black-and-white now, I still see in color.

From this kaleidoscopic landscape emanated a sense of peace, a spirit of satisfaction, of contentment, feelings I longed to take back to San Antonio with me to exchange for the city's soul-grinding anxiety and paranoia.

The village boys here were nothing like the tattooed neighborhood gangs of San Antonio, the thugs who always looked like they were figuring out how to shoot you in the face and have time to grab a pizza afterwards. Here, the streets were nothing like San Antonio's blaring mess of flashing lights, squealing tires, car stereos at decibels that'd blow grandma's laundry off the line, everything awash in that ubiquitous TV-blue glowing from everyone's windows. In San Antonio, stuff just made noise, took up space, had to be paid for, had to be fueled. It was one giant conveyor belt, with the community running just to keep up.

Night and day, a mere sixteen hours from Texas.

As George and I soaked up all we could from the village and its way of life, we began to wonder if we could apply any of what we'd seen to the situation back home. By the time we wound up on the coast at Puerto Vallarta a couple of weeks later, we were anxious to get back to San Antonio—and start changing things. We wanted to make it a more pleasant and safe place to live, to create programs with neighborhood rebuilding, landscaping, and streetscaping at the top of the priority list. The Mexican beer talking? Maybe. But we knew our ideas were valid.

George stayed behind in Puerto Vallarta so he could drive his father-in-law back to the States. I took an Aeroméxico flight, and in a few hours was banging on Armando's door with a satchel full of Mexican snapshots.

My friend Armando, born in San Antonio, was a painter of Mexican

*Jesse Trevino
my ultimate hero*

heritage. He looked just like Zapata, but without the funny hat. Armando was a local hero and had been since his portrait was used on billboards back in the '60s to promote Coors beer to Mexicans. In the '70s, he made the papers by presenting the Pope with an oil portrait of His Holiness . . . still dripping wet. Later, he was arrested when he painted one of the Market Square oak trees with industrial strength enamel in fire-engine red. He'd recently discovered a Belgian painter's work, a centuries-old series of paintings with red trees in them. If Armando had had a taller ladder and another day or two to work, he probably would've painted the whole tree, including the leaves, solid red. His art wound up drawing attention to the city's plan to cut down trees for more parking; residents pitched a fit and the city kept the trees.

George and I had begged Armando to come with us, but he didn't have any money or proof of citizenship. He'd been to the border towns and hated them, as I did. Now I couldn't wait to show him the real Mexico—the boulevards of Guadalajara and the mountain village with the waterfall and all of the color, color, color. Mexico's color. My color. Color for me was a whole new life, and no one would understand this better than Armando, with his paint-spattered hands and paint-smeared clothes and murals ablaze with high-test hues. If I could just get him to answer his door.

When he finally came to the door holding a tumbler full of red wine, I immediately wanted to get as drunk as he was. He invited me in and we helped ourselves to his several cases of beer and endless supply of restaurant wine.

The more we drank, the more I couldn't shut up about the color. Armando knew exactly what I meant: how the people in Mexico seemed to have appeared like flowers from the earth, how they fit right into the whole circle of life, how they seemed in tune with God, with family, with nature. How, in Mexico, there were music and pretty girls in every corner, every hamlet, no matter how isolated. We talked until three in the morning, and then I fell asleep on Armando's couch, an old Army cot draped with a couple of Indian blankets.

I woke the next morning to Armando's "Grinnnnnngo!" as he walked into the studio with a bag full of breakfast tacos and paper cups of steaming Mexican coffee. He cleaned off the metal kitchen table and dried it with an old towel. We spread the photos out as we ate. "These are beautiful," Armando said as he munched. He wanted copies.

After breakfast, Armando rolled the worst-looking joint I'd ever seen, but we managed to smoke it without setting ourselves on fire. Then he brought in a box of oil paint tubes and some knives. I yanked a couple of ice-cold beers from the fridge, and before I knew it Armando was smearing raw oils straight from the tube onto one of my favorite shots. And before I could tell him how this would never work, it was working. Armando did some of his best painting that day, daubing and smearing on little 4x6 Mexican snapshots. The colors were so intense they seemed to vibrate, and the pictures took my breath away.

When Armando's paint was dry, I took the pictures over to Jesse Trevino's

Yellow rose of Texas

Mariachi Plaza
Guadalajara, Mexico

Mexico

Mexican on bench (left)
San Antonio

Red rose of Texas

Guadalajara, Mexico (left)

Man with cotton candy
Mexico

MEXICO

A WORK OF ART

Armando painted my color print then we enlarged and hand-lettered it

studio. Jesse was another artist friend of George's and, in a way, Armando's rival. The two artists couldn't be more different. Jesse does one or two paintings a year, usually sold before they're even done, and he gets thousands of dollars for them. Armando, on the other hand, works like a man possessed for a couple of weeks, and then does nothing for the next two. Armando is spontaneous, reckless, exciting. Jesse's thought-out and meticulous. I love them both.

Jesse liked my Mexico shots, and the raw oils Armando had knifed onto the prints got him talking about his country. "Mexicans take color for granted," Jesse said. "But I grew up in Monterrey, and what I remember more vividly than colors are smells. Inside every house, people were cooking or making coffee and tortillas, all day long and into the night."

Jesse'd come to the U.S. with his mom when he was just a kid, after his dad died. In San Antonio, his mom showed a Catholic priest some of young

Jesse's drawings, the priest contacted some art educators in town, and within weeks Jesse'd acquired what amounted to scholarship funds to attend a local school for the artistically gifted. Later, he landed a full scholarship to the Art Institute in New York City. His first year there, he received his draft notice.

Some of Jesse's friends pointed out to him that since he was born in Mexico, he didn't have to go to Vietnam. But Jesse willingly packed his bag and headed for boot camp, telling his mom that America had been good to him, and if America needed him to fight, he would fight. His twelfth day in-country, he stepped on a land mine, which took out large pieces of his knee. As the mine's blast tossed him into the air over a rice paddy, machine-gun fire ripped Jesse's right arm off at the shoulder.

After a year of surgeries and another year of rehab, Jesse came marching back to San Antonio with U.S. citizenship, a Purple Heart, the Medal of Valor, a metal leg brace, and a wooden arm with a stainless steel hook where the hand used to be. He moved into his mom's back porch and for three years kept the curtains closed, drank whiskey, and felt sorry for himself. Then he emerged as if nothing had happened, and started all over. He signed up for art classes at the local junior college and learned to paint with his left hand. It was a tough struggle, and by the time he could make halfway decent paintings they were no longer the classic art school portraiture of European royalty or cloudy day landscapes. Now Jesse was painting gritty San Antonio neighborhood scenes of shops, bars, and gas stations—his childhood memories of Texas. Every line was deliberate, realistic.

From Jesse, I learned what a treasure it is to be American. Being an American by choice, like he is, showed me, an American by birth, how special this country really is. Eventually, the Smithsonian bought one of Jesse's paintings, the museum's first acquisition of Mexican-American art.

I could tell Jesse loved the painted snapshots Armando and I created. And it meant more to me than I can say.

The Mexicans showed me color, and I have never been the same.

Armando
painting my photos

Rocky Mountain Way

Smokey Wendell has been Joe Walsh's personal assistant since 1974, the days just after the death of Joe's first child in a car accident, way up in the mountains above Boulder, Colorado. Joe'd just finished his solo album *The Smoker You Drink, the Player You Get*, "Rocky Mountain Way" was a landslide radio hit, and Joe was in the process of gathering more material for another solo album that was going to blow everybody's socks off. He had this great house up in the mountains, a precious little daughter, a wife who was a real ballerina from a blue-blood Boston family. Money was rolling in from the James Gang's hits of a few years before, there was coke everywhere, a studio in the basement—every day was New Year's Eve.

Smokey was summoned from Detroit to help Joe keep the business straight. The sky was the limit. Walsh was gonna give Hendrix a run for his money, and since Smokey was ex–Secret Service, he was just the guy to protect Joe from the nuts and bolts of the music biz. It was a Kerouac-meets–Norman Rockwell world up above the clouds. And no one expected anything would ever go wrong.

When the housewife in her truck banged into Joe's wife in her truck and snapped their daughter's neck, killing her in an instant, suddenly the Shangri-la became a hellhole of misery and heartbreak. And there to hold all the broken pieces together was Smokey, the designated adult.

Throwing handfuls of coke out into the snow, arranging a funeral, restraining Joe and his wife from suicide, selling off the mountain hideaway to which neither parent could return—there was Smokey. The wife fled to Boston and walked away from the marriage, and Joe went crazy for about ten years.

Smokey stuck it out at Joe's side no matter how drunk, how late, or how off the wall things got. At one point, Joe was living in a camper in the alley

Joe Walsh at home
Boulder, Colorado, 1975

behind a Los Angeles recording studio, getting up most mornings to drive to the city dump and shoot rats. Day after day, for nearly a year, Smokey would go to the studio and cover for Joe. "He's working on new material," he'd say. Smokey'd check the mail, return the calls.

He saw Joe through rehab, joining the Eagles, getting his career—wounded as it remains—back on a track of some kind. Smokey and Joe are both old millionaires now, addicted to five-star hotels, room service, and retread families.

I joined Joe and the Eagles on their "Long Run" tour in 1980. Broke as usual, I'd gone to Birmingham, Alabama, where my uncle owned a construction business that built high-end custom homes. To increase his market share, he'd bought a cul-de-sac in a blue-collar neighborhood, and the scheme was for me to supervise the building of five inexpensive houses at once. Halfway through the project, the Eagles came to Tuscaloosa, just a two-hour drive away.

Joe invited me to come down, maybe shoot some pictures, so at noon on a Friday I headed out in a construction van to the University of Alabama. There was an all-access pass waiting for me in the production office. I wandered around the basketball arena where guys were setting up equipment on a stage that wasn't yet completely built. Janitors were covering the hardwood court with rolls of thick black rubber padding and setting up folding chairs.

Walsh hit the stage at 4 PM and plugged his guitar into a small Fender amp. One by one, the other Eagles showed up and plugged in. Joe, looking like a high school music teacher, shouted out, "'Barefootin'—in a one, two, three, four." It sounded dangerous right off the bat. Walsh brought a raw

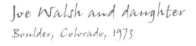

Joe Walsh and daughter
Boulder, Colorado, 1973

sound to the Eagles—that gritty guitar of "Life in the Fast Lane" and "Hotel California," plus the *Long Run* album—and the other band members seemed to want to show their rough edges too, at least at the soundchecks I witnessed on that tour. It was at these afternoon rock-a-thons that the Eagles played down and strip-bar dirty.

That night, I took pictures backstage, onstage, and backstage again after the show, and then I drove back to Birmingham. The Eagles were off to play Atlanta and Jacksonville before heading to Dallas, where they'd home-base for a string of shows in Texas and Louisiana. The group had their own plane, so they'd do a show, and then fly back to the Anatole Hotel in Dallas, which they called the "Ayatollah" because of its over-the-top architecture.

Joe called me from Atlanta, wanting to know if I'd printed up enough pictures to show the band. I had, so he arranged for me to fly to Dallas and check into the hotel. I brought a footlocker full of mounted, matted, and retouched black and white 11x14s and began setting up a darkroom in the bathroom to process new prints. When I'd gotten the darkroom roughed in, I found Joe's room number from the list Smokey'd included in my room key envelope. Joe answered on the first ring.

"What room are you in?" he said. "I'll be right down. I've got a surprise for you."

Two minutes later, there was Joe at the door.

With Karen.

She looked like Paris-meets-Tangier, all the way down to her extremely high heels. We weren't a couple anymore, I hadn't seen her in two months, and I was stunned.

"How long have you been here?" I asked, squeezing her like she'd just won the Miss Universe crown.

"I live here, silly," she said. "Remember? This is where I fly from. You write letters to me here." I'd almost forgotten she was now a Braniff flight attendant.

It felt weird, her coming in, following Walsh around. Did she call him? Did he call her? Maybe she'd just bumped into Smokey at the front desk and asked to see Joe. Or maybe Joe'd told her I was flying in any minute, so now she was acting like she came down on the off chance I'd be there. Maybe. But more than likely, maybe not. I was still glad to see her, even if hanky-panky seemed to be playing in the distance.

I went back to setting up the darkroom and Karen helped me place some photos around the room. We put some on the wall using wadded-up masking tape and after a while, it was a virtual pop-up gallery of the Alabama shots I'd made the week before.

The race for soundcheck was about to begin—whoever got there first chose the songs—and Joe wanted us to ride in the limo. He wanted me to bring the pictures. I grabbed a stack, and when we got to the venue Karen and I put a few on the wall in the main dressing room. The rest we arranged across the white tablecloth of a catering table. The shots, just a few days old, looked cool and needed no explanation. The band approved.

Glenn Frey had been the first at soundcheck and was sitting at the piano.

He wanted to do Ray Charles's "Lonely Avenue." Don Henley sang Ray's part and the rest of the Eagles were the Raelettes. It started out as a piano tune, but wound up as a guitar tune, thanks to Walsh. Unforgettable. I managed to get that on cassette.

Karen stuck around for the first couple of days then flew out on an overseas flight to Europe. I traveled with the band, four shows in six days, flying around Texas in their rented turboprop jet complete with two Dutch attendants who were drop-dead gorgeous.

The best part for me on an Eagles tour always came about thirty minutes before show time, when the band found a place to sing. In these big sports halls, more often than not it was a large tiled shower room, nice and echoey. Glenn Frey'd strum an acoustic guitar and the band would sing tunes from their *Desperado* album—"Tequila Sunrise," "Doolin-Dalton," the title track. They sang loud and pure, warming up their voices, getting in sync. The sound was sheer Eagles-in-the-shower beauty.

The Eagles were perfectionists. Still are. Henley is the Pavarotti of West Coast rock, giving each show everything he's got, including serenity. Even back then, their approach was to make the show sound just like the record, only better. They have so many hits, though, that it takes two hours just to play most of them. That's always about forty-five minutes too long for me. Still, the Eagles in concert today are as good as it gets—and worth every penny.

The shows in Texas were huge, sellouts in giant indoor venues. I'd never seen so many beautiful women in one week. I thought the chick situation

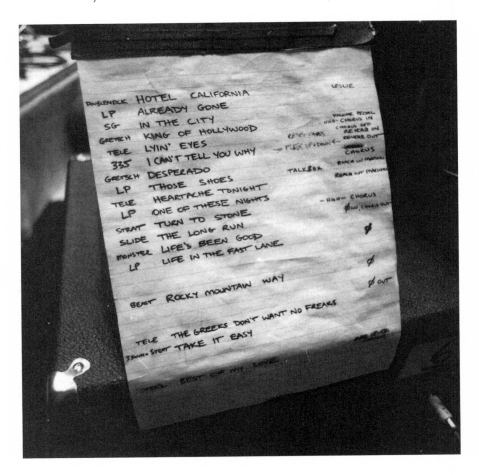

Eagles set list

Don Henley
Long Run tour
Baton Rouge, Louisiana, 1980

was outrageous with Rod and the Faces, but the Eagles had hordes of gorgeous women continually swarming them, even chasing the limos down the freeways holding up signs that read "Do Me" or "I'm the Best." It was bad-boy heaven. And in this case all the bad boys looked so sweet and were exceptionally handsome. Except Joe, of course, who looked like laugh-'til-you-choke trouble.

After the Texas dates, the band headed for L.A. and I flew back to Birmingham to finish the houses. The first one went on the market the same day the Iranians took the embassy hostage. Mortgage interest rates zoomed to eighteen percent, with balloons that went higher, and my moneymaking hopes in the building business came to a screeching halt.

I drove back to Austin flat broke and rolled into town on empty, a tape of *The Long Run* playing in the van the whole ride. The more I played it, the better I liked it.

I've kept in touch with Joe and Smokey over the years. Not long after my 2006 trip to England for the Who Convention, Smokey sent me an email, wondering what was happening. I thought I was telling him, tried to explain, but it was like I was dumping crude oil in his gas tank. "You went to England and Pete Townshend was making you tea? I don't get it, but good luck anyway. . . ."

CHAPTER THIRTY

Faces

The Faces blew through San Antonio during the late summer of '75. It would be their last tour. After the show, I drove frontman Rod Stewart, keyboardist Ian "Mac" McLagan, and guitarist Ronnie Wood—drummer Kenney Jones had fallen for a tall cowgirl backstage—in my dark bronze '38 Chevy with a Corvette engine to an oversized bar and restaurant I managed over on the north side, now my "real" job since the grants had run out. The joint was San Antonio's first fern bar, a clubhouse for yuppies that held close to 600.

As we were driving, I suddenly realized that no one had ever actually ridden in the back seat before. I'd bought the hot rod real cheap from an Air Force guy who needed the money, figuring it wasn't too much of a splurge; after all, I had the real job now, for chrissakes. The ride's interior was far from finished, though. Just under the dash you could see wires and paper tags, and if you looked up all you saw was raw metal. But from the outside, it looked like some badass show car.

I wanted to apologize for the funky interior, but the guys were all chattering excitedly about the show at the Municipal. It had been a capacity crowd, about 2,500, the perfect concert size. The Faces had been phenomenal; they took the place over halfway through the first song and held on 'til the last note of the last encore.

Rod was in the back seat, and as the afterglow giddiness subsided, he started to sing. The car windows were open a little; the metal roof put a mellow echo on his vocals: "I don't need / No more rock 'n' roll ladies / All I need is a six-door Mercedes." He sang the lines over and over, repeating them different ways. Just before it seemed like it might turn into something, I pulled up at the loading dock around back of the restaurant.

My first Faces photo shoot
Ann Arbor, 1970

"Saved by the sound of the pails," Mac chuckled as he stepped out of the front seat near a dozen trash cans and a dumpster.

I ushered the band through the back door, and then kept them standing in the huge kitchen. There was plenty of room. My kitchen staff, dressed alike in white chef coats and hats, was from all walks of life, but I didn't have to explain to them who the freaks in the flashy stage gear were. They knew. The Faces were superstars.

I ran out to the dining room floor and rounded up a few of my referee-shirted waiters to form a makeshift security force.

"I've got Roddy-Poo and the boys in the kitchen," I told them as we huddled like a football team, "and as soon as the stairs are clear, I'm gonna walk them up." I turned to one of the bartenders. "As soon as you see guys in satin pants hit the stairs, start ringing that tip bell," I directed. "Pretend you just got a hundred dollar tip 'til I get them upstairs."

I herded the band from the kitchen, trotted them through the very back of the dining room, and then up the stairs. Patrons who saw them—or at least the hard-to-miss satin trousers—didn't believe their eyes. Others who'd just come from the concert didn't seem to care that the Faces were all headed upstairs, together, to where the restrooms were located.

On the second floor, I opened the security door to the attic, which was outfitted with an old grand piano, a three-piece drum set, darkroom, shower, john, and a recording room where I made tapes to play in the restaurant. There were a few couches. Booze? You name it.

Faces tour
San Francisco, 1974

Mac took a seat at the piano. It wasn't in tune and a few of the keys were dead. Ron found my guitar and tiny amp. Rod paced around the room aimlessly, occasionally singing along with the music from downstairs coming up through the floor. When the whistle blew for last call—at 1:45 AM—a waiter brought up a tub full of ice, some Guinness, and a couple of bottles of Blue Nun for Rod.

After a while, Rod called for the limos; the Faces were flying out later that morning. While we waited, Shultz, a waiter who was turning tables at the restaurant until his rock dreams came true, brought up his bass and mini amp that he kept in the trunk of his car. Greg, a bartender who owned the drums, strode in with a couple of sticks and brushes in his back pocket. Within a couple of minutes we had a full-blown jam going: Chuck Berry tunes one after another, Rod belting out "Reelin' and A-Rockin'," "Johnny B. Goode," "Memphis."

Soon the limos arrived. Mac wanted to stay, so I walked Ron and Rod down the stairs, back through the kitchen, where they both signed the apron of the Mexican girl who cut up the tomatoes and onions, and then out to the first of the waiting stretches.

Back upstairs it was Mac at the piano, bartender Greg using brushes, and Shultz playing tasty bass. Mac pounded out blues for half an hour, while I made cassette tapes with a recorder on the floor and made sure he never lacked for Guinness.

"I think the band is about to break up," Mac suddenly blurted out during

Rod Stewart
Detroit, 1970

a lull in the music.

"What?" I yelped. That hurt. "You can't do that!"

I was utterly astonished. If the British Invasion had fired the rock revolution's opening salvo, the Faces were the occupying forces bringing up the rear. They changed things for the better. Their discography read like a well-spent musical life.

"The Stones call Ron every day," Mac said, "and Rod wants to move to L.A. and go solo." He shook his head slowly as he fingered the keys. "One thing I know is I can't make it as a blues piano guy. I never play this stuff unless I'm around you."

He rolled out a few more riffs, sighed, and then stood up.

"I must shove off, mate," he said, brightening, and giving me a friendly clap on the back. "It's been lovely, but we're off first thing in the morning. I'll tell Kenney about your place."

"I'll call you," he said as he climbed in the back of the remaining limo.

Faces
mid-'70s

And he did—about ten days later from Miami at three o'clock in the morning. He was crying and swearing.

"It's final. They're both leaving. We've got four more gigs and then that's it, it's all over. I can't believe this. Can you come out with us and take some Last Supper pictures? We're here tomorrow night. I'll buy you a ticket."

There was no way I could leave; it was the weekend and we did twenty grand worth of business on Saturdays alone. I asked Mac where the next

Rod Stewart
Las Vegas, 1974

four shows were. Memphis, Chicago, Detroit, Montreal, he told me.

I hadn't missed a day of work since I'd started at the restaurant. But, hell, this was the Faces.

"I'll see you in Chicago," I told him.

Montreal. The last show. A five-tier ice hockey arena, circa pre–World War II. Looked like a giant bowler hat. Problem: no one could find Ron Wood.

The place was jam-packed, every inch of four balconies shoehorned with French Canadians, screaming, yelling. Down on the floor, the ice was covered with thick plywood and thousands of upholstered folding chairs. But no one was sitting. They were all standing, holding plastic cups of beer, impatient, unhappy.

It was forty-five minutes past show time. The warm-up act, a new Canadian girl band called Heart, had finished their set. The crowd was getting louder

Ian McLagan,
Ron Wood,
Rod Stewart

and louder, hurling insults in French. It was on the road to getting nasty. Even the chicks in miniskirts in the front rows were miserable. "Snappers," the band called them. During a show they'd be banging their knees together as if they were fanning their insides, drop-dead gorgeous flashers trying to get the band to stare at their underwear, or lack thereof. And nine times out of ten the ones without underwear were smooth snappers. You know what I mean—everyone's favorites. But Ronnie's delay tonight had the front row skirts holding their kneecaps together; the roadies and stagehands were getting nothing.

Thirty miles away, Ron, reeking of liquor from his all-nighter back in Detroit, was in the clutches of a rent-a-cop, detained when his tiny chartered prop plane had dropped him at some private airport. To get himself up for the show, Ron had spent the short flight smoking joints and snorting piles of cocaine. When he tumbled out of the plane in flamboyant stage clothes—beer in his hand, nose smeared in white powder, guitar slung over his shoulder like an M-16—the rent-a-cop practically pissed his pants with joy. Here was the Drug Bust of the Year.

Back at the arena, the mayor of Montreal, seated amongst the snappers in the front row with his daughters, had the rent-a-cop on the horn. "We're on the verge of a mass riot!" he barked into the phone. Lives were at stake—including his own. He ordered a motorcycle police escort to carry Ron Wood backstage pronto.

Some skeptics hold that the Faces' drinking made them a sort of lovable, but sloppy band, placing them in the same category as the disoriented and drooling Jim Morrison or the redneck, brawling Lynyrd Skynyrd. Those critics are way off base.

The Faces drank, no doubt about it, but not to the point of sloppiness. I've seen a hundred shows, soundchecks, late-night jams. "Sloppy" is a word that doesn't fit anywhere. It would be like calling the kid who can ride his bike with no hands, shoot you the finger, and yell something all at the same time a sloppy rider. The Faces were so good they made it look easy.

Aside from pocket flasks, there was booze on the planes, booze backstage, and plenty out front. Eventually, the band even had the roadies build and stock a bar onstage, complete with a bartender who'd pour refills atop the amps and next to the drums. Rod went for his beloved Blue Nun or champagne; the band pretty much stuck with Jack Daniels and beer. Whenever there was a break in the vocals, Rod would wander over to the bar, have a word with the bartender over a glass of bubbly, and then sprint back to the mic—never missing a beat.

Rod Stewart
Chicago, mid-'70s

Rod didn't smoke pot. He said it screwed up his voice. Kenney, the Faces drummer who'd eventually take Keith Moon's place in the Who, said it messed up his timing. But everybody drank. And these were the years when things went even better with coke, man. Doctors would show up with vials of pharmaceutical uncut flake and say that there was nothing bad or addictive about it. It kept you going, no matter what. In exchange for a blizzard, the doctors could hang in the dressing rooms and mingle with the girls, who, by the way, were everywhere.

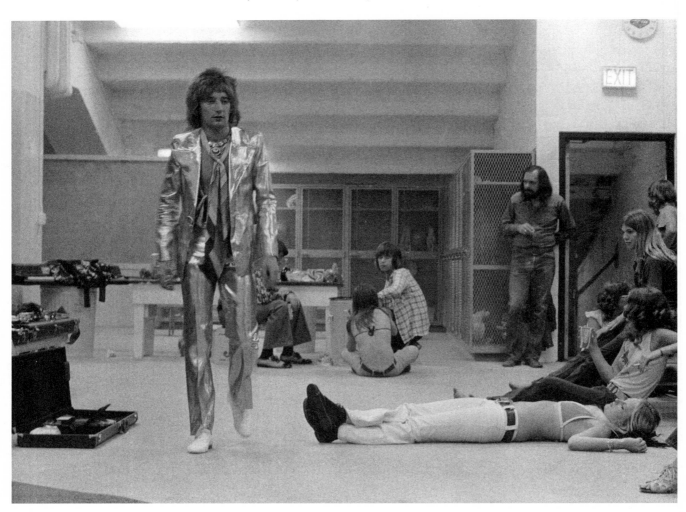

Rod Stewart
Tulsa, Oklahoma
early '70s

My experience with coke was haphazard. It was so expensive I never bought any in my life. But I also can't remember ever turning it down. People who had it would carry it around like a tin of Russian caviar; if something really special came up, well, it just kind of topped things off. The roadies dug it because they could keep working and drinking. Bands liked to do a few rails before the show and maybe during breaks. It wasn't really until the mid-'80s that the seemingly harmless Peruvian marching powder started to show its real face. Then things got ugly. Guys who'd been doing it for years came unglued and turned paranoid, and then pretty much null and void.

Whenever the Faces came to a town, the most beautiful women within a hundred-mile radius would swarm the hotel, descend backstage, jam the front rows. Girls loved coke, so local promoters, deejays, rock doctors, and

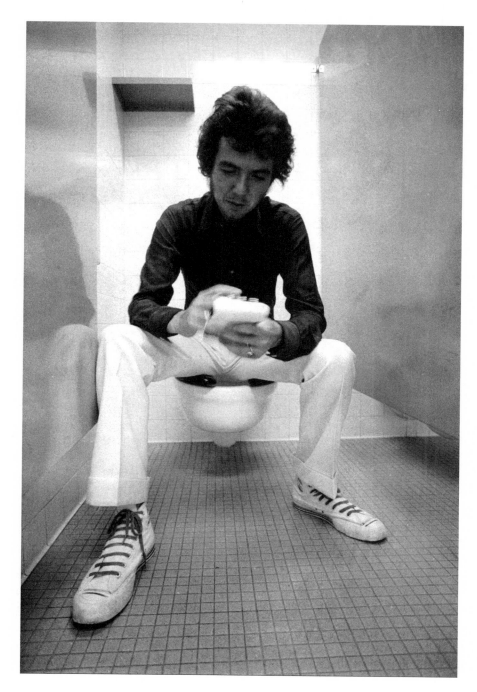

Ronnie Lane
Faces tour, 1972

sleazy lawyers gave it away by the shovel-load just to hang out with the band. Every town had a cluster of these people, who all knew each other. They gave each other passes and intros and wound up mingling with the band.

I'm not sure I ever even tried street coke. Doctors had pharmaceutical pure stuff in little brown vials smaller than a lipstick tube that held an ounce of squeaky-clean flake. If you dumped out the vial on a mirror, it would fluff up. It looked like someone had just knocked over a sugar bowl. Sniff up a couple of rails of that, and they could yank out your front teeth and you'd keep right on talking. Strung-out models would come backstage, snort up a bunch, blow everybody, and then walk away still looking like they'd just stepped off their *Vogue* cover from the month before. But by the time people who could afford it couldn't stop, it had moved mostly out to Malibu or back

Faces tour 1975

to London. There the snorters sat with the curtains drawn, counting and recounting their dwindling record royalties.

The Faces had always maintained the we're-all-in-this-together-we're-a band-it's-not-Rod-Stewart-and-the-Faces-it's-the-Faces line. The reality was something entirely different. The band may have started off as a unit . . . well, sort of. The Small Faces had lost their singer, Steve Marriott. Rod needed a band. But Rod had become maybe the greatest singer-performer of the whole era.

Rod had sung all his life, first around the house and then in his parents' pub, in skiffle bands and pub rock bands, eventually singing for guitar god Jeff Beck's band. Rod basically did three things: he sang, he allowed himself to be chased by women, and he played soccer. That was it. He was in peak athletic condition and was still being pursued by professional football teams in England who hoped he'd walk away from a string of hit records and become their soccer savior, which he surely could have been.

The band, on the other hand, was used to Marriott, a pragmatic lead singer who could also compose and play capable rhythm and lead guitar. The Small Faces had had plenty of hit records before they'd even met Rod. They didn't see themselves as backup guys, but rather as English royalty who'd allowed Rod to join in on the good life. They forced him to work his way up. But by the last tour, Rod was the focal point of the band, whose name had been shortened to the Faces when he'd joined. He'd grown into a truly exceptional performer. Fast, graceful, he kept things moving as only an

Rod Stewart and Ron Wood
1972

athlete could. By then, he'd sung so much, so hard, that he had full control over his vocal rasp, even at full volume, something he'd never mastered with Beck. Later, with Rod's solo smash "Maggie May," the public decided they liked his gravel-throat and the notes that just barely landed on key.

Ron Wood had come to the Faces from the Jeff Beck Group, as well, so the two new guys were a team within a team. Because of Rod's and Ron's looks, their ambition, and their talent, they were gaining serious altitude in the music world, and the Faces as a band began to fade out of focus. But the band gave Rod his edge. Night after night, the Faces would nail your ass in your tracks; they could turn an entire arena into a giant English pub, ripping your heart out because they looked the part and sounded better than their records. For the people who bought tickets, the Faces were as good as it got.

And Rod made the band look good. He'd gallop all over the stage, coaxing the very best out of them, singing right in the other guys' faces. And he brought new cachet to the lowly mic stand. Whereas Elvis had danced with the mic stand like it was a mop handle, Gene Vincent had grabbed and fumbled it like an exhaust pipe he was trying to tear from a junked pickup, and the Beatles barely even touched the things, Rod would strut by a stand and grab it like it was the neck of some cheap gangster, yank it up to his lips like he was singing into the hapless guy's ear, and then upend it like a weapon to fend off an onslaught of pissed-off boyfriends. Rod was everything at once, a harmony of rock and roll spirit, athletic showboating, and sexual electricity. All the while, the chicks in the crowd exploded, not screaming so much as sex-throes moaning. The Faces took it all in stride.

American bands had a tendency to get buzzed and belligerent; the Faces

Faces
Los Angeles, mid-'70s

All endings are unexpected, but this was as powerful a blow that one could imagine. Don't push back the pain. Welcome it in, examine it. Every thought will be carefully turned over like a coin and stared at, memorized. Then another thought will push its way in—welcome it. Eventually, you outlast the pain and the thoughts that come to you are calm, loving reassurances from Kim who had a wonderful life and went straight to heaven. You both are adjusting.

It's tough. But I know and love you, Mac, and you can take this. It's not a punishment, it's a look at the scale of life . . . grief . . . loss . . . passing . . . in full-volume pain.

You will make it through.

Love,
Tom

Ian McLagan
early '70s

Grit Kids and Keith's Bust

CHAPTER THIRTY-TWO

In the late '70s, I was living in Austin, Texas, down on Fourth Street in the warehouse district, sharing everything but the rent with friends from the San Antonio art school, a posse that included Steve Humphrey, the pottery artist-in-residence. The warehouse was huge. Steve had built a huge kiln in the vacant lot next door, the front portion of the building we'd transformed into a gallery, all white, painted brick that would've held its own on Fifth Avenue or the Champs-Élysées. Behind the gallery, I built a darkroom, and beyond that was the pug mill where the potters mixed their own clay. They got so good at it, they began to market their mix to schools. Soon they were so swamped with orders that they had to hire a full-time clay mixer. So, for ten hours a day, this guy created clouds of clay powder, an unending dust storm just feet from my darkroom. I wound up working only at night, after the dust settled.

I'd sold a photo feature to *Texas Monthly* and done some portrait work, along with the occasional band shot. But mainly, I was simply absorbing the city of Austin—and loving it. It was a small town then. Willie Nelson was the local guy making a name for himself, drawing attention to Austin, and especially its music.

The university was in the middle of town, next to the capitol grounds, and nine months a year the town was flooded with college students, not just from U.T. There were five other colleges in Austin and lots of trade schools, so naturally there were bars everywhere, cool little places that'd attract the students. And music was how the war for the beer dollars was fought.

When Willie Nelson performed at the Armadillo, he'd pack the place, break all beer sales records, singing his hit "Blue Eyes Crying in the Rain." The Fabulous Thunderbirds, Stevie Ray Vaughan and Double Trouble, and Lou Ann Barton worked the bar circuit. Austin's favorite touring band was ZZ Top. You didn't have to search for good music; it was everywhere. The hot radio station was KOKE.

Keith Richards
San Antonio, 1973

At the warehouse, we worked as much as possible, drank as much as possible, smoked as much as possible. Our motto was, "We have everything but money—and it's worth it." The future would take care of itself.

Then the phone rang.

It was Harry Phillips from Detroit, Mitch Ryder's organ player. A couple of years before in San Antonio, I'd helped Harry with a demo tape of some of his original stuff. Now Harry was calling from Russ Gibb's house. They wanted me to come up.

Seems they'd bumped into each other in a bar, started rehashing old Grande stories and lamenting that the place was closed and falling down. Russ had just returned from London and told Harry about the next new thing, punk, which sounded awful but looked cool, with loads of energy and attitude. As they kept drinking, Russ—still a teacher, despite his phenomenal success as a concert promoter—started talking about going to a teachers' conference in Washington, D.C., and reading in the papers there about a pocket of white hillbillies living in areas in Virginia that were now surrounded by black neighborhoods, which meant constant trouble and nonstop fighting for the kids. For protection, these white kids, who called themselves "Grits," had formed loose-knit gangs. Their agenda was pretty simple: leave us alone.

Russ was so intrigued he wound up driving through the neighborhoods. He spotted Grits all over the place. They were young, just barely in their teens and, like the punks in England, loaded with tattoos. The Grits looked different than their hillbilly or hippie parents, sporting khaki slacks rolled up past the ankle, sleeveless white undershirts, and spotless white tennis shoes. They combed their hair with Brylcreem and worked on being tough, not hip. Smoking pot was considered a weakness; Grits drank and tried to be like James Dean. Their music of choice? Fifties rockabilly.

Russ stopped and talked to a few. Hardly any went to school anymore, they told him. At sixteen, most everybody dropped out, patrolling the neighborhoods and malls instead. When Russ asked about the '50s look, the '50s music, one kid explained that the '50s weren't coming back, they'd just never left. "Hippies are cool," the kid told Russ, "but Grits rule."

I could tell Russ thought he'd tapped into the future. Before he and Harry had left the bar, he'd hatched a plan to form a real young band and rehearse them 'til they were hot, and then fly back to Virginia and grab one of these real Grits off the street with the tough, tattooed Elvis look to front the band. He'd call them the Grit Kids. Harry suggested Russ fly me up from Texas to produce a demo, something with that certain twangy, tangy sound that I seemed to pull from musicians. The plan was to throw a band together, make a hot demo, get a huge record advance, and live happily ever after.

Luckily, when they phoned me in Austin, I was between binges, and though staying at Harry's meant unrolling a sleeping bag atop two footlockers on the back porch with Scar, Harry's Doberman, it sounded like a fun project. We all thought we'd be rich in ninety days.

In reality, it was like reinventing the wheel using a Rubik's Cube. When I'd left Detroit almost ten years before, every kid in town was a rock-and-

Grit Kids
first stage rehearsal
Detroit, 1977

roll something or other. Guitar players were everywhere. When I returned to look for kids to mold into rock stars, they were all playing tennis or Pac-Man at the mall. Aside from Harry's kid brother, who'd gotten a drum set for Christmas, we had nothing. It took four months of ads, auditions in the living room, and notes thumbtacked to the bulletin boards of every music store in a fifty-mile radius of Harry's house to finally find four kids who fit the bill.

I'd arrived broke and now I was really broke. But the guys we'd assembled—average age, fifteen—were totally committed. Even with school starting up, we were getting thirty to forty hours of rehearsal out of them per week. What made it intoxicating was that the kids became committed to each other, the four teenaged parts becoming a whole, and every rehearsal was 100 percent better than the last.

Drunk and high at the piano late at night, Harry would come up with "pockets," riffs or melodies or hooks. I'd stumble back to the porch with Scar and scribble out words or refrains that fit the pocket. Then we'd crash 'til the kids got out of school, stay sober while the parents sat in the kitchen or went shopping, and work with the kids until way after dark. The boys were making Grit Kids T-shirts on their own. We were all sure this was gonna be a hard day's scam.

About this time, Harry got a call from Chuch in Paris. The Stones were taking a break from recording in France and were gonna meet up in Toronto to start the tour. He was flying straight to Detroit and wanted to know if he could crash at Harry's for a few days to get blasted and hang out. Chuch had been Ron Wood's guitar tech from the Faces days, and when Ronnie joined the Stones, he brought Chuch with him. Chuch was making lots of money and flying all over the world.

When we collected him at the airport, he was ready to get ripped and hear all about the Grit Kids project. It was Saturday and the kids would be showing up soon for rehearsal. They arrived to find a guy from the Rolling Stones' entourage, fresh off the plane from Europe, here to listen to them. For the kids, it was almost as good as a record contract. Unlike the hours, days, and months it took the Stones to get fired up enough to actually play, the Grit Kids hit the living room running, plugged in, and started playing as soon as they walked in the house. They were good; everybody could feel it, including the parents. They played for hours—Led Zeppelin, Cream, ZZ Top. Chuch was blown completely out of his socks.

He flew out that Monday to his home in Michigan's Upper Peninsula. He had a couple of weeks to rest up and get ready for the Stones tour, but he called us every day. Eventually, he told Ron Wood about this smoking band of extra-young kids hoping for a record deal. Ron wanted us to bring him some tapes and photos in Toronto. The day before the Stones were due to arrive in Canada, Chuch called with some incredible news.

"Man, you're not gonna believe this," he said, "but the Stones have booked and paid for a month in a twenty-four–track studio here that they're not gonna use. The album was finished in Paris, so all they're gonna do in Toronto is have stage rehearsals in an airplane hangar."

Breakfast with the Stones
San Antonio, Texas, 1975

"So what does that mean?" I asked.

"What it means, for fuck sakes, is that Ronnie and Keith said you can drag those kids up here and record on twenty-four tracks for a fucking month. And it's free."

We called for a family pow-wow and told the parents the great news, that the Kids could record in a plush, state-of-the art studio on the Rolling Stones' dime. Harry and I would go up to Toronto to get set up, we told them, and then we'd return for the kids and we'd all drive up together. The parents froze. "What about school? My son's fourteen—I don't want him hanging out with the Rolling Stones. Well, I don't know. . . ." It took until midnight to get the parents to sign off on the trip. It was agreed that the guitar player's dad would rent a van and bring everybody up after Harry and I called with the go-ahead.

Next morning, Harry and I set out in his Volkswagen bug loaded with cassettes and pictures of the Grit Kids. We were ecstatic. Our plan was to meet with Ronnie and Keith and try to talk them into getting involved with the Grit Kids. It was all becoming so real, we could taste it.

Then, about an hour south of Toronto, we heard it.

A radio announcer broke into programming to say that Keith Richards had just been arrested at the airport with "enough heroin to keep every addict in Toronto high for a week." He was in jail, along with his longtime girlfriend, Anita Pallenberg, who de-boarded the same airplane wearing a sun hat with a fried egg on top—a real one.

Harry almost drove into the ditch.

We stopped at the first gas station and called the Grit Kids guitar player's house. His mother answered and told us in no uncertain terms that her son would not be coming to record with Keith Richards, and she'd talked to the bass player's mom and she wasn't going to let her son hang out with heroin addicts, and they both were thinking of pulling their kids out of the band. Harry and I got back on the road toward Toronto. We wanted to at least thank Chuch for offering the big break. We also wanted to see what would happen to Keith; like they'd said on the radio, Keith could get up to twenty years for trying to "smuggle" in that much raw heroin.

We arrived in Toronto the next morning and called Chuch from the Stones' hotel lobby. He was up, everybody was up. Keith's English lawyers, who'd spent the night on a transatlantic flight, had retained some Toronto lawyers to spring Keith from jail on the basis that he had a sold-out concert to play that night. The possibility of backlash from cancelling a Stones show, something that could be perceived as political revenge by a jealous prime minister, whose young wife liked to hang out and get high with the Stones. Well, that was enough to get Keith out on bail, along with his goofy, loose-lipped girlfriend.

And now here we all were, in this huge hotel lobby, the Royal something or other, right on the water. The Stones, the Stones' crew, the management, the lawyers, the PR people, the wives and girlfriends, spread out all over the restaurant, which took up most of the lobby. All the other tables were filled with the groupies that always flew in, like the girls who followed the fleet, along with Canadian police—plainclothes and otherwise—American DEA guys, and lawyers and reporters filling in the gaps.

"Keith must be really scared," I said to Chuch. "He could do some serious jail time here. This could be the end of the Stones."

"Scared?" Chuch scowled. "All Keith's worried about is that he's out of heroin and every cop in Canada is watching him eat breakfast. He's not scared. He just doesn't want to do a show without getting blasted."

Harry and I didn't stay for the concert. Keith's heroin bust was on the front page of every newspaper, and the Grit Kids project hung in the balance. But we did catch soundcheck that afternoon, which, with the Stones, was as good as it gets. The band was as edgy as I'd ever heard them, raw and loud, mostly to burn off tension, but also to fry all the law enforcement that'd wandered into the darkened theater, lurking behind the seats and under the balcony. It looked like a scene from a Peter Sellers Clouseau flick: cops from every walk of government work all waiting to take the stage, seize more drugs, and read some more warrants.

The Stones seemed to be playing for their lives as a band. And Keith was playing like he was out for blood, not from the cops, but from himself for being so stupid. He might survive twenty years in prison, but not without broken fingers and a busted face. Guys would beat him up just for the notoriety. Keith Richards belonged out here, onstage. Any stage. Left to his own devices he'd play all the time. Like Hendrix, Keith took off the guitar just long enough to change clothes or sleep, which wasn't that often.

Harry and I stayed to hear the band start with "Miss You," move through "Hoochie Koochie Man," and then do fifteen minutes of "Brown Sugar." It seemed like the stage was gonna burst into flames, there was so much energy and slice, like a firing squad audition. As the Stones downshifted from playing to standing around, Harry and I jumped back into the black Beetle and headed for Detroit. If we didn't get hassled at the border, we could make it to Harry's by two in the morning. It was four in the morning when we got there. A phone message was waiting for us. Russ wanted an 11 AM meeting tomorrow, which was now today.

It was the end of the project, we were sure. We'd make the meeting and, as they say, face the music. Harry set every alarm clock in the house for 9:30, went upstairs, and fell onto his bed fully clothed. I flaked out on the living room couch so I'd be ready to walk out the door, and, most importantly, so I didn't walk out of the house smelling like his dog Scar.

The alarms all went off and we were on our way, sure that Russ would read us the riot act and then dissolve our music company. I'd be lucky if he didn't cancel my return ticket back home to Texas. But when we got to his house he was positively giddy. He wasn't pissed at all. Instead, he saw the Keith Richards debacle as a reason to call a press conference and make a big deal out of the enthusiasm the Stones had showed these kids. We'd spin it that the Grit Kids' management thought it would be a negative experience to meet some real-life rock stars who were, according to the newspapers, not opposed to heroin. As if we'd saved a band of innocents who were, by the way, the Next Big Thing.

Firefall
Criteria Studios
Miami, 1976

This was the kind of stuff that would get the band noticed, at least in the papers, Russ enthused. Then he'd send the press clips to the record companies and start the pre-bidding buzz. Russ was beside himself. And it turned out just like he predicted. The Detroit newspaper came out with a huge *National Enquirer*–type piece, and Russ was the hero, of course, with the executive directive to protect these talented kids from rock star drug addicts. Russ was able to raise more money, shore up parental support, and keep the rehearsals going. By this time, five months into a six-week project, the Grit Kids were as hot as a blowtorch and so much fun to watch. Sheer youthful exuberance. And the band could rock.

Not long after, a group I'd shot an album cover for, Firefall, was booked to play Pine Knob in Detroit, one of the most beautiful outdoor venues at the time. I'd kept them up to speed with the Grit Kids, because the teens were doing Firefall's strongest tune, "Sharp Shootin' at the Senator." The day of the Pine Knob show, Russ chartered a helicopter, picked up the Firefall guitar players after soundcheck, and landed in Harry's backyard. Russ made sure reporters and photographers surrounded the house as the Firefall guys sat in on a Grit Kids rehearsal. When that story hit the papers, we were good to go for a few more weeks of rehearsals. We kept it going 'til there wasn't one more penny anyone could spend. In the end, the vacuum that Russ had sensed and hoped to load with the Grit Kids was ultimately filled by other things. Deborah Harry was the sex goddess of the New Wave, the Sex Pistols were the bad boys of punk, and the Grit Kids had no place to go after school so they just waited for a call.

CHAPTER THIRTY-THREE

J. D. Souther

1977. Patrick Cullie was with the Eagles full-time, serving as an assistant road manager or accountant, something that required a briefcase and that they paid him for. I, on the other hand, was living in my parents' garage in San Antonio.

Patrick called me from Chicago. "Hey, you want a little job? J. D. Souther just finished his solo album and he's going out for six weeks. I'll still be out with the Eagles and can't do the tour, but these guys will take my word for it that you're up to the job. What do you think?"

"Who the fuck is J. D. Souther?" I asked as I looked around the garage, photos strewn between flowerpots, stacked amidst wine bottles. I was back in San Antonio with not much to do. The only area of my life in which I was making any headway was my chosen field by default: drinking. I didn't have an income. I didn't need one. My new stepfather was successful in the restaurant business and had simply told the maids to make sure I got food out in the garage. I set up my darkroom, the restaurant drivers delivered wine and beer by the case when I called them, so all I needed was cigarettes and gas money.

"Souther's a songwriter," Patrick said. "Everybody loves him out in L.A." He filled me in on the rest: that Souther'd lived with Linda Ronstadt for years and wrote a lot of her hits; that because of her, Souther met the Eagles, who were her backup band; that J. D. hit it off with the Eagles. They were all the same age, all smart, talented, and out on the cutting edge of the L.A. music scene. Souther wound up writing and co-writing some songs on the first Eagles album, and co-wrote most of *Desperado*. Patrick definitely got my attention. I just wasn't sure.

"I don't know," I told him, "it's been a while since I've been on the road. And, besides, I wasn't much of a road manager when I was doing it." Six weeks of commercial flights and rent-a-cars? My knuckles went white just thinking about it. And there'd just been a big plane crash, a loaded airliner

Bill Graham and son
Los Angeles, late '70s

headed for L.A. from Mexico City. After a rainy takeoff, it'd flown right into a jungle mountainside.

I told Patrick I needed a day to think about it, that I'd call him in the morning. I sat down in the corner of the garage, drank a couple of bottles of rosé, and conked out. At 4 AM, I woke up in the same place I'd slumped over ten hours before. Without thinking, I started packing.

The J. D. Souther band was just starting rehearsals and Patrick had said that I should make it out as soon as possible. When I called Patrick back later that day to tell him my decision to take the tour, he told me he'd already informed the managers to expect me. The L.A. office had me set to fly out of San Antonio at five o'clock the next afternoon. Patrick would meet me in L.A. and get me squared away and introduced to Souther, the band, and the business managers.

I was packed, the ticket was at the airport, and I could buy whatever film I needed when I got to Los Angeles. I had a free day and a fridge full of restaurant wine. So what that I didn't own any Linda Ronstadt records and my son had taken my copy of *Desperado* with him when he'd gone back to live with his mom? So what that I didn't know much of anything about Souther? What the hell—I'd road managed the Who, the James Gang. I'd dragged Patrick into the Hard Corps after college, his wake-up call to the world of music . . . with a degree in English lit. I wasn't worried about anything but the flights—six weeks' worth.

So, once again, I drank myself to oblivion on the floor of the garage. I dreamed my fright flight dreams—the emergency landing with the Who, the ride to Cleveland on acid—then woke up at four the next morning, drank some more, and dozed off 'til noon. When I woke up, reality started to close in. The rain that had started last week was still there, and now there was thunder and lightning. An omen? I hoped not. But that little voice that usually said things like, "What the hell, you can open another bottle," and "You expect more from the Corps," was now saying things like, "Don't do it. Fly around for six weeks? You're crazy!" and "You could die just as easy as not." As I drank some more, I answered the voice with, "Yeah, I don't even know these people" and "Fly around with a bunch of strangers playing Linda Ronstadt tunes? Right."

But in the end, I went, only because Patrick had put his credibility on the line vouching for me. I was dropped off at the airport, picked up my ticket, and headed straight for the bar, where I switched to bourbon and ginger ale, one after another. Then I read the fine print on my ticket: I'd be flying on an L-1011. I thought those were grounded because the back doors kept blowing out and making the plane explode. Great.

I switched to doubles. In the course of trying to get brave, I got really drunk. When it was time to board, I sat in my seat, buckled up, and stared out the window. Though it was late afternoon, it was so dark and overcast it looked like the middle of the night. The moment of truth came; we roared down the sloshing wet runway. Suddenly, the engines cut back from full blast to idle, and we seemed to skid sideways, as if the plane was sliding into home plate. Then it jerked to one side, leaned over, and stopped. To my drunken mind, we were obviously moments away from seeing waves of jet fuel in the aisle, our last memory before the explosion. Actually, we just rocked once or twice and came to a slanted halt.

The right landing gear had slipped off the edge of the runway, the captain announced reassuringly, and we'd be getting towed out of our predicament. Like when your car slides into a ditch, I guessed. After an hour of flashing lights outside in the rain, I started to feel trapped. After all, we were on the main runway of a major airport and now it really was dark, and raining like hell.

Eventually, we were evacuated, put on buses, and taken to the airport hotel, where it was explained to us that they didn't have the proper equipment to pull the huge airplane back onto solid ground that night. After the hotel bar closed, I located my luggage in the lobby, went to my room, and watched replays on the news of the plane sitting crippled along the runway. My last thoughts as I passed out on the bed were that this was an omen and there was no way I was getting back on that aircraft.

The world looked different in the morning. The sun had come out, the plane had been moved, and I was on standby for any of the next six flights leaving for L.A. I took the Southwest flight at one and Patrick met me at the airport. He'd arrived the night before from Chicago. Together, we headed to Souther's management office on Hollywood Boulevard, but none of the bigwigs were there. Everyone had gone down to SIR Studios for rehearsals.

My heart sank as I walked in. Souther was a small guy, about the size of your average high school sophomore. His red-bearded face, though, was definitely *Old Man and the Sea*. He was standing in front of the band with a Martin D-12 slung over his shoulder like a rifle and he'd just taken prisoners. The band was silent; Souther was yelling. As Patrick and I moved toward the stage, Souther stopped, smiled, leaned down, and shook my hand so firmly it hurt.

"Thought I was gonna have to run these assholes myself," he said. "What a relief. Welcome aboard."

The rehearsals went on for a few more hours. The music, at first, was depressing. This wasn't rock. It was more contemporary California, you-had-to-have-been-there music. If you were rolling in money, with lawyers and strung-out fashion-model types lining you up with endless cocaine rails, this was what you'd listen to. If you'd been drinking for a month and living in your stepfather's garage, on the other hand, this music was pure B-grade Muzak—songs not even good enough for elevators. And the band looked like they'd been recruited from the waiting room at the drive-thru car wash. I knew that if I didn't go down in a Buddy Holly ball of flames, I'd definitely be earning my money on this tour.

Souther just strummed his guitar, songwriter chords played mostly with his thumb. It sounded okay, but the lead guitarist was right out of Juilliard with a major in lounge lizard jazz. It wasn't just a weird combination, it was downright awful. The keyboard player was unpleasant to watch and listen to, as well. They just sounded unfixable.

In the midst of this audio-visual hodgepodge, Souther's voice was an entirely different story. No wonder the Eagles liked this guy. Every time he opened his mouth, it sounded just like that group, a little bit of each of them, all the harmony parts, combined in one voice. It was obvious that this was where the Eagles had gotten their phrasing. The more I heard Souther's songs, the better I liked them. I wound up taping all the shows and soundchecks on the tour.

After a few days of rehearsals, the band was scheduled on the red-eye to D.C. to play the Cellar Door in Georgetown. Patrick had given me a metal briefcase chock full of airline tickets, vouchers, hotel reservations, rent-a-car account info, and the tour book with all the phone numbers from every town for everything we'd possibly need. Compared to the Who, the Faces, the Eagles, or even the James Gang, this tour was tiny. But there was still the same pressure to get things done. And once it started, it was the only thing of importance in my world. All I had to do was be the travel guide, rent-a-car driver, and keeper of receipts. I could hear some songs, shoot pictures as they happened, and have constant access to wine and drink.

I didn't realize it until a few years later, but I was entering a phase of drinking where I was imbibing all day, every day. On our days off, I stayed in my hotel room, printed pictures, and *really* drank. For me, alcohol was now an essential ingredient of everything—including vodka and orange juice with breakfast. But, remarkably, I could still function. Even though I was drinking nonstop, I also drove—everywhere.

Functional drinking, I'd learn later, is a phase that can last for years. To maintain some semblance of a normal life, to plan and solve problems in spite of the drinking, I'd go over and over stuff all the time. I'd write stuff down, look for pencils, watch the clock—all things were urgent, all the time. Some people got yelled at, some got a pat on the back, but whatever the circumstances, I was determined that the gig would happen, the band would get paid, and we'd move on to the next show. This was about the time that the frown became permanent. I was frowning all the time. Trying to remember. Drinking to forget.

So the tour was okay. J. D. did a lot of radio interviews for his new album and talked about all the songs he'd written for other people. Most of the gigs were at small, hip clubs in hip towns, where the people were so hip that they often passed on shelling out ten bucks to see Souther. So unless it was a college campus show, the band was playing to fifty or a hundred people a night, which hardly covered our expenses. Looking over the receipts toward the end of the tour, I saw we'd taken in five grand, and spent close to a hundred.

But this wasn't like the old days, when the tours had to pay for themselves. This was forty little conventions in which Souther was to win over the tastemakers, get people talking and buying the record. It worked, kind of. The tastemakers loved him, everybody was talking about him. But the record didn't sell. The reason: it was no good. It was filled with great songs, but they were executed by L.A. studio guys who played all that California deadpan-'cause-we're-so-high-tech rock of the '70s. Flawless, yes . . . and utterly soulless. Still, most people who saw Souther live probably still

Elvis Costello and the Attractions
first tour, Austin, Texas

remember it. If he'd done those same gigs by himself, he would've become a legend.

Calvin "Fuzzy" Samuels, Souther's black bass player, was originally from Jamaica but had lived in L.A. for ten years and was proud of both. He'd become cool in L.A. ever since he'd worked on some hit records with Steven Stills, like "Love the One You're With," and he was the first of Souther's band members that I'd gotten to know pretty well.

Heading for Dulles International and the first gig in D.C., the band was scattered all over the plane. Fuzzy was seated in front of me, and J. D. was up in first class. He paid for the upgrade himself; he loved to fly with the well- and high-heeled. He didn't do first class to belittle the band; it was more just to supersize his flight experience. Besides, he was an L.A. songwriter, not your basic rock musician. J. D. was above the fray.

I wasn't. Just as I got my briefcase open on the fold-out tray, the smoking light went on, so I lit up a Camel. I saw Fuzzy lighting up a cigarette too. In an instant, I got a huge whiff of Jamaican ganja. Then I saw a mushroom cloud over Fuzzy's head, the odor of pot unmistakable.

Fuzzy'd taken the tobacco out of the front of his Kool and stuffed in about three good tokes of weed. It was pretty clever. With the first drag, the other passengers' first thoughts would be, "No, that couldn't be possible." By the second drag, people would think it's probably one of those no-nicotine things. And by the third puff, when folks were saying to themselves, "That's pot, that's all that could be," Fuzzy'd be down to the tobacco, and a once-over by the stewardess would reveal only a Jamaican guy smoking a filter-tipped Kool.

Meanwhile, I was frozen in terror in the next row. Those two guys in suits seated next to Fuzzy could've been Secret Service, DEA, FBI. We were flying to Washington, for chrissakes. I folded up the new metal briefcase, ever so casually slid it under the seat, closed the tray, shut off my reading light and pretended to fall into a deep sleep. To this day, I don't think even Keith Moon or Keith Richards would've done something so blatant—and I was thirty minutes into a six-week tour. I needed a drink, but waited 'til the smoke cleared to ring the stewardess bell.

Souther's piano player was also a graphic designer, who, when he wasn't touring, worked in a small ad agency in L.A. designing logos and writing jingles. To pass time on the road, he'd take down the framed artwork in the room and painstakingly razor-blade pictures in the same colors out of porn magazines. Then, using spray glue, he'd fill the mundane watercolors with the nastiest, raunchiest porno shots you ever saw, reconstructing the artwork so that, at a distance, you'd never know the difference. It was only when you leaned in close that you'd see it was laced with porn, which, in many cases, actually improved the overall look. They're probably still hanging as he left them.

Fuzzy and the black drummer would sit in Fuzzy's room, watch TV and smoke pot all day. Souther would be locked in his room or rooms, singing and writing songs. If his girlfriend—a sitcom actress on *Welcome Back, Kotter*, who'd fly in and out for a few days at a time—was there, they'd set up a rice cooker and vegetable juicer in the room and make a point of eating organic and vegetarian. If she wasn't there, Souther'd just order Chinese delivery. If the hotel had a good menu, Souther'd order a top-of-the-line steak.

Souther's dad had been a musician in some big bands, and he came out to a few gigs. Both of these guys were hotel connoisseurs, always talking about the so-and-so in Miami and how that compared to the Palmer House in Chicago or the Plaza in New York. And they both loved to fly. When J. D. discovered I was a reluctant flyer, he set out to get me to embrace it. "I like the idea of speed," he told me, "knowing that I will be somewhere totally different in a few hours." To which, I'd say something like, "Yeah." Once I said, "We could blow up on takeoff." "So what?" Souther replied. "It's not like you'll miss anything, like you'll miss any of this." I wondered if he was right.

Six weeks and nobody died or got arrested. Management wanted me to fly out to L.A. with the band to go over stuff, but Houston was too close to home. I made Xerox copies of all the receipts, express-mailed them out, and then drove the rent-a-car to Austin. I was ten pounds lighter, had a few paychecks in my pocket and a couple on the way, and felt like I'd made it out of my stepfather's San Antonio garage. This was Austin, and even though I was no longer employed, I felt like I was on a roll; I convinced my few friends there that I was.

After I got settled, I called home to San Antonio to check in. My sister, who'd married British band manager and Stiff Records co-founder Jake Riviera, was now in New York. Jake was about to leave on tour with Elvis Costello, former London pub-rocker turned New Wave artiste.

Costello'd be rolling into Austin in a week or two and my sister asked if I could take some fresh group shots of the band. She wanted me to hop on the tour bus with them and get some live shots, as well. Though I'd never heard of Elvis Costello, I was a professional now, and since it was my sister, of course I agreed.

Just before Costello came to town, I read in the newspaper that a California songwriter, ex-boyfriend of Linda Ronstadt, had demolished his new $100,000 sports car on Mulholland Drive and was in the hospital. Looking at the photo of the demolished car, I couldn't figure how anybody had made it out of there alive. The article went on to mention that "New Kid in Town," which J. D.'d written with Don Henley and Glenn Frey, was becoming a huge hit for the Eagles. Souther'd have plenty of dough to repair the car.

I was just guessing, but it seemed to me that Souther's songwriting would save not only a totaled car, but a totaled tour that would've wiped a lesser talent right out.

Seemed Souther really was above the fray.

Jake and Elvis

The late '70s and early '80s hit me and my generation hard. Anybody who'd ever been important was now washed up, dead, in jail, or in hiding, and not much was happening musically.

This was the void into which Jake Riviera leaped and created an empire.

He'd gone to L.A. from England on his own, didn't know a soul, but he'd done his research. He started showing up at the offices of A&R guys at the major record labels, Elvis Costello demo in hand. His English accent and aggressive charm got him in the door; when he played the tape for the hotshots, they ushered him right back out.

At that point, Jake would lay it on full-strength: "Look at you, cushy job, cocaine residue on your nose, and all those cute little things in the front office. Why, you're so burned out and screwed up waiting for the next big thing that you don't even know it when you hear it. Elvis Costello is so hot in England and Germany right now that they say he's gonna be bigger than Dylan. And there you are just sitting on your ass. You don't know what's hip anymore. The only thing in your future is probably a drug bust. People told me you were losing it, but I just thought I'd try you first. Now I see for myself."

Then he'd storm out of the office—making sure he'd left his business card on the desk—and slam the door.

It was brilliant, really. By planting the seeds of career doubt, insinuating that everybody knew about this or that guy's drug problem, and reminding the bigwigs that their record company was one of the thirty-five major labels who'd passed on the Beatles fifteen years earlier, in just three days Jake had stoked paranoia and launched a major bidding war to sign up Costello.

Jake flew back to London, held an audition, and put a band together in one day. He knew what he wanted in his musicians—lack of experience, no other prospects. Easy marks to sign complicated, binding contracts on the spot. "Take it or leave it, mate," was Jake's big mantra. It worked.

Jake Riviera
Austin, 1978

Jake was one of the first English band managers to take Austin seriously as an important musical city, and not just for Willie Nelson country acts. When the Elvis Costello tour bus rolled through town, I climbed on board. It wasn't long before I wanted to jump off.

Elvis's idea of fun on the bus was to listen for people talking on their CB radios along the highway, like kids trying to chat with truckers. He would grab the mic and cuss them out, use obscenities, call them fuckups on the air. It took me about an hour to get him to stop, and it defined him permanently in my mind as totally low-class. Then there was his infamous comment about Ray Charles. Asked about the singer, Elvis was quoted as saying, "He's just another blind nigger."

I lasted just a few days on that tour. I couldn't stand the music, except for "Allison," which I kinda liked. Elvis was a goofball. Jake was the powerhouse, and for him I did Elvis posters, Nick Lowe album covers, and a Dave Edmunds EP cover.

Jake and my sister had been married in my stepfather's house in San Antonio, where I'd been living in the garage when I took the Souther tour. My stepfather had Jake's parents flown in from London. They stayed in San Antonio for about a week and loved it. Jake and my sister bought a house in London; their marriage lasted ten years. After I got out of rehab, I went over there and shot pictures of *East Side Story*–era Squeeze keyboardist Paul Carrack, and did some more Nick Lowe stuff. After Nick Lowe married Carlene Carter, June Carter Cash's daughter, I took pictures of her as well, since Jake was trying to launch her into the mix.

I admired Jake's gusto, but this wasn't what had drawn me to music. In fact, just hearing about it, or the music itself, was painful. It seemed to me that all these guys wanted to be big stars and travel around and act snotty and get rich; they just didn't want to rehearse. As a band or a group of people, they just didn't seem worth spending any more time with—sister or no sister. I reached my quota real quick.

Some of my notes from that tour did wind up in my own lyric box, though: "You could scandalize your neighbors / You could move outta town / Change your name to Elvis / And call it underground . . . "

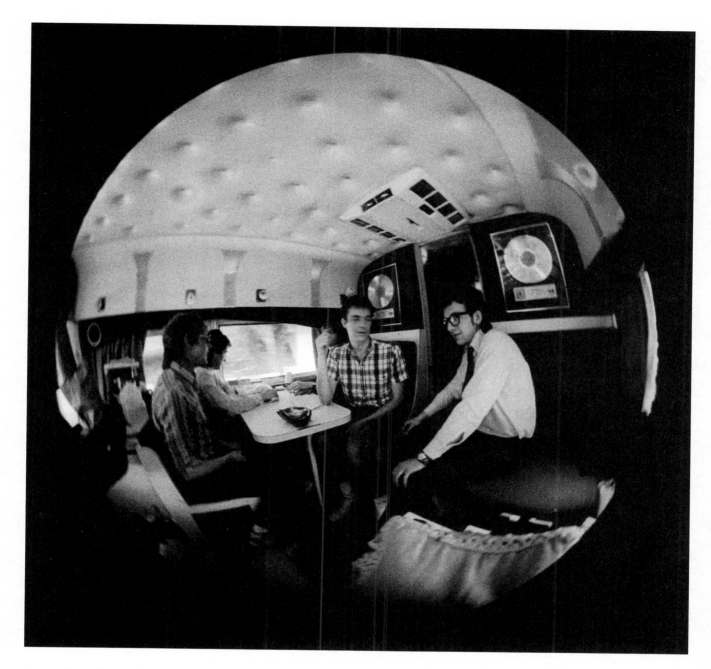

Snapshot from hell
the first Elvis Costello tour, 1978

Cassette Recorders and Soundchecks

A handheld cassette recorder has been a part of my carry-around stuff since they came out in the early '70s. The first one I'd ever seen was given to me by a guy from Sony. He'd come down to the hotel in L.A. and passed them out to Rod Stewart and all the band members. Since I was with them, the guy gave me one, too. They were packaged in a little black cloth briefcase, and came with two speakers, headphones with small sponge-foam earmuffs, and an adapter so you could plug it in the wall. The big thing, though, was that these recorders ran on batteries and had built-in mics. For the next few weeks, we sat around on airplanes listening to tapes through our headphones. The other passengers and flight attendants were amazed, and wanted to know where we got them and how much they cost.

The whole concept of a portable, personal cassette recorder caused commotion everywhere; no one had ever seen anything like it. But for a traveling band, it was a natural. Six months later, they started showing up in stores. It was damned clever marketing. That Sony guy back in L.A. probably handed out hundreds to touring bands, who would, in turn, travel around the country showing off Sony's new toy.

Early on, at one of the soundchecks, I put a blank cassette in my machine, hit the record button, set it down on a chair a few rows out, and basically forgot about it as I shot a few rolls. By this time, I'd learned that soundchecks were far more exciting than the shows, simply because there were no rules.

At a show, a set started with this song and ended with that one, and if they brought you back out, you played this and this.

For the Who, soundchecks were infrequent. Roger would go down and check the mic; maybe Pete would show up, maybe not. Keith, at three in the afternoon, was usually in recovery somewhere.

The Eagles, on the other hand, would race each other to soundcheck. Whoever got there first would pick the tunes, and they rarely had anything to do with the show. It was more like "Stump the Band." They'd do "Barefootin'" or "Memphis," tons of old bar band tunes. When the Eagles did them, just pulling them out of the blue, they'd sound spectacular. Even if the guys had never played the songs together before, or couldn't remember the words, they'd fake it. It was breathtaking how good they were, even when they were goofing around.

When Rod Stewart arrived at soundchecks, it looked like a schoolboy field trip. He'd walk right up to the mic and start singing at full volume, while the

Rod Stewart
Chicago, 1977

sound guys out in an empty auditorium would scramble with dials and the band guys would strap on guitars and start playing. It was always fun and, most of the time, funny. They'd fool around until the band sounded tight, and then they'd just jam for a half an hour. Afterwards, we'd all head back to the hotel pool and goof off until show time.

It was poolside where I played that first soundcheck I'd recorded on my new Sony. I plugged in the speakers, spread them out on the deck chairs, and let it rip. The sound was phenomenal, crystal-clear stereo. The built-in mics had picked up the sound of the auditorium, so, unlike the recordings the sound guys made from plugging into the mixing board, the cassette I'd just made sounded like a real live recording. It had a presence and ambience that the technical guys' recordings didn't. I was hooked. So was the band. The guys would bring their recorders to soundcheck and get me to make tapes for them.

The whole question of how people got wrapped up in cassette machines is sort of like asking what the world was like before cell phones. I can remember driving down the highway, watching for a restaurant or gas station with a phone booth, trying to call somebody 100 miles away to tell them that you were lost or late, dealing with long distance operators and handfuls of quarters, reading the graffiti inside the booth while handling a greasy, filthy phone that hadn't been cleaned since it'd been installed. Some things, when they come along, just fit, and you wonder how you ever got along without them.

On that first headlining Who tour that I road managed in 1968, we had a rented bus, a driver, a roadie, the band, and me. I was responsible for everything, and part of my job was to keep track of the money—all of it. This I did with spiral notebooks and pencils. Every day I'd stand on the bus with piles of receipts spread out on a bunk, adding hundred of numbers, and doing it twice, just to be sure. After a few weeks of this, I convinced Chris Stamp, the band's manager who'd call me from London every day, that I needed an adding machine. In those days, an adding machine was almost the size of a typewriter, and you had to buy spools of paper and bottles of purple ink—a nightmare, basically. So when calculators came out later that year, there was no big adjustment period, no hesitation. Compared with a calculator, the adding machine looked like an Army tank. It was immediately dumped.

Just as the calculator was to the adding machine, the handheld cassette machine was to your dad's giant reel-to-reel tape deck. The handheld cassette recorder was made for rock and roll. Song ideas, messages home, live recordings, playbacks on airplanes—once I had my hands on my first one, I never let go. I've kept them around to this day.

CHAPTER THIRTY-SEVEN

Divine

Divine, Texas is thirty miles south of San Antonio, and, as late as 1984, was stuck somewhere in the *Summer of '42* era. I leased an old bank building from the '30s, abandoned for the last twenty years, and moved in. I went down there because the rent was a thousand dollars less per month than the same size place in San Antonio, but the longer I stayed, the less of a bargain it seemed to be. I hoped it wouldn't take long to sort through all the bullshit I'd been carrying around since 1962. I never knew what to keep and what to throw away, so I stored, hauled, and lugged boxes, trunks, and mostly footlockers everywhere I went. Now I'd brought them to this godforsaken collection of rooms in Divine to open them up and confront all the bizarreness.

A general system developed. I put all the photo equipment in the walk-in safe, all the paperwork in the front room, and I lived in the middle, along with the paintings and the bicycle. There was no hot water, so boiling water on the stove, taking it into the bathroom, and pouring it into the huge, stone-cold iron tub became my version of the Sisyphus myth. But at the end of the day, the tub wasn't quite full of lukewarm water, and I was soaking wet from twenty-two trips to the bathroom with the steaming bean pot. A metaphor of my life at that point: why bother?

I knew that if I categorized all my photos, tapes, notes, clothes, and equipment, I'd be back at square one at the moment in my life when I should be finishing up something like a career and enjoying a big savings account. On top of the world, as they say, a guy who really knows what he's doing. But I felt like the only part of me exposed to the real world was the tips of my fingers, poking up out of some dark, damp drain, and that when the light was just right you might get a glimpse of my eyes—timid,

Self-shadow portrait
somewhere in Texas
somewhere in time

quiet—just taking up space, sewer space. And by dying I'd produce a bad smell, and my contribution will have taken place.

I was forty years old before I'd ever heard people talking seriously about their "careers." It was something that just never came up. The people I was with thought, "Let's get real toasted. Let's just get fried. And then we'll go to the gig." Everybody assumed that, anywhere along the line, we'd all be thrown into solitary confinement, our passports would be lifted, we'd be penniless and humiliated, our families would be embarrassed, and we'd be in jail forever.

If someone had told me back in '62 that I'd be living alone, smoking cigars, and watching my hair fall out when I was forty, I probably would've blown my brains out. The only difference between my lifestyle at that point and the one I lived twenty years earlier as an art student is that I had less pot, less snatch, and I didn't have a record player anymore. I still slept on the floor, I still had no money, I still smoked. I just had more wrinkles and less hair.

Me in rehab
Austin, Texas, 1982

I couldn't even listen to music anymore for longer than about five minutes. I'd switch it back to talk radio—small talk radio—forty-five minutes of what the coach of the Boston Celtics was really trying to do, fans calling in to suggest he was losing his touch, maybe he's stressed about the playoffs or it has something to do with his contract option. Then news would break in for a minute: another 500 added to the Union Carbide death toll, some more Ethiopians dropped dead, but before they died they said it wasn't a conspiracy and to tell those guys in New York thanks for that planeload of "tax deductible" high-heel shoes they sent, really hit the spot. Problems, problems, problems, and then the South Americans didn't even appreciate that we sent gangsters and cutthroats down there armed to the gills, just to keep it interesting. The government says there will be no recession. They repeat: no recession. Then back to the Celtics, thank God.

Annie Leibovitz
backstage, Who tour
1975

So there it all was, in Divine, Texas.

I do confess to liking the name. To anybody who's never been there, it probably sounds kind of cool. I just wished it was thirty miles south of Paris.

The goal in Divine was to separate my life from my work. The snag, of course, was the definition of each. What is my work? What should my work be or have been? What should my life be? What is the purpose of the work? What is the purpose of my life? Big deal, right? Obviously, he who must ask has already missed the point. 'Round and 'round, like a mouse stalking its own tail. Should the mouse bite the tail off? Or debrief himself?

And, by the way, I wondered then, what the hell does debrief mean anyway? Shortly after the hijackers were taken into custody, the hostages were flown to Washington for debriefing. "Welcome, gentlemen. We have to explain to you why you can't speak to the press, because here's what's really going on, and so, you see, national security is at stake, and, of course, we don't want you to say anything." "Excuse me, sir, but how long has Grenada been known for its school of medicine? What the hell are Americans doing down there studying medicine? Is it the voodoo perspective, or is it the fact that it's just a hop, skip, and a jump from Haiti? And since we all know the number one Haitian export is cadavers for American medical schools, they just set up a place downwind from the United States to carve up bodies. What did they do with the leftovers?" Time for some more debriefing.

Pick a subject that no one has ever heard of, a country and a dilemma that doesn't exist. Then announce on the radio that "according to recent polls, the majority of American people favor blah, blah, blah." The next day, conduct an actual poll, and you'll find that the majority of Americans really do favor blah, blah, blah. Have you ever met anyone who was polled? What about debriefed? Did Hitler debrief the Jews? Were the Jews debriefing the Arabs? Were the Arabs debriefing the Jews? Could I go out in the job market and become upwardly mobile after I got polled and debriefed? How about a video game called the Midlife Crisis, a multiple choice test of what to do with the rest of your life? Winner gets polled. Loser gets debriefed.

The radio, the TV, on all the time; my surrogate family chattering away. The glue that holds society together.

I'd lived in the Divine building many times before in different cities in different decades. The high ceilings, the crumbling plaster, the way the wind shook the windows late at night, the old fixtures and bare overhead light bulbs. It was an "old" place fifty years before I arrived.

But it was a step up from where I'd just been, crawling through the brink of rock-bottom. Were it not for my van, I would've been homeless. When the tags expired, I parked it at a friend's house and stayed in his garage, drinking a case of beer and a half-gallon of wine a day, passing out on the gravel floor. At least it was softer than the floor of the van.

No, I was at home there in Divine. No phone, no family, no mail, no income. It was all I could do to get up and sort. The first few minutes, I'd fight the urge to set the whole thing on fire. It was all garbage. It was all an anchor, its historical significance just possibly a chemical imbalance in my body. Full documentation of opportunities wasted, people used and discarded.

Karen was crying on the phone.

"I'm still a crybaby," she said, "but, Tom, you're going to have to do something about your pictures. Because if you don't, you can bet someone will. I think about it a lot. I've pictured myself coming down there, like one of Picasso's old girlfriends, to get your pictures out. I thought that when you quit drinking, you'd change. But it sounds like that's not the case."

She stopped crying for a moment.

"You know," she continued between sniffles, "I don't even really count your rock pictures. I mean, pictures of Rod Stewart and Pete Townshend are fine, but the ones I remember are the ones of Europe. The nuns in the rain. I still remember all those pictures, and when I look at the one on my wall, it's as though I can hear them chattering away in French."

"You have a copy of that shot?" I asked. I couldn't remember giving her one.

"Yes, a reject. But I can remember the one you kept."

I could hear her wiping up with a Kleenex. Then she laughed. I listened.

"You may not know this," she said, "but my best friend died last year. She was only twenty-nine. We had the week off and went to New York. We were walking down the street after lunch, about a block away from the hotel, and she started to look real strange. I asked her if she was all right, and she said she was just getting a real bad headache. So we sat down on some steps for a few minutes. I thought she'd snap out of it. But after we sat there for a while, she said she couldn't see. I flagged down a cab and got her in the back, we raced to the hotel and she got sick all over the cab.

"After I got her up to the room, I called the ambulance. It got there in just a few minutes, but by the time she got to the hospital, she was in a coma. And by nine o'clock the next morning, she was dead. Can you believe it? Twenty-nine years old. She had a brain aneurism, and just like that, she was gone. I had to go tell her folks. She was my best friend, I loved her dearly, and she just died. I'll tell you something: it changed my life completely. I know now that the same thing could happen to me. I could die tomorrow. And when I start thinking about that, I can't help but think that, by all rights, you should've died years ago."

We were both silent. I was digesting her story, savoring her tone of wisdom. She was grown-up now. She was eighteen when I met her, now she was thirty-three. We lived together for over ten years and had been apart since '79, and I believe we managed to break each other's hearts.

A week later, Mary Ann called.

It was Tim. He got drunk.

My own flesh and blood, drunk at fourteen. Mary Ann wanted me to talk to him. What could I say? Tim, you must not drink so that you can keep yourself together, so you can grow up, get a job, get an apartment, get a boat, and then drink and drive around in circles like half the population of Florida? God, how I wished she could've told me that he had sex with the maid or something. A lot of people think drinking problems are in the genes; he got everything else, he could've gotten that one, too.

Drunk. So that means he's not afraid to drink, maybe smoke pot, maybe sniff coke, and then get on his three-wheel ATV or play with his gun or something. How about drunk on his bicycle? Drunk on the skateboard? What about his heart condition? What about if he gets drunk and his heart beats out of control? And there's Mary Ann, with the same heart condition, and she drinks.

And Mary Ann's husband, the son of the owner of the real estate office where she worked after she left me, he drinks. She hit me with divorce papers, married him, and, voilà, landed her nice house in the nice neighborhood with, you guessed it, the white picket fence. Trouble in her paradise began when she found out this guy drank as much as I did. Only when he got loaded, he wasn't even funny, just stupid.

Tim, drunk. It was too much reality.

Forty-two and counting. I couldn't believe it. In the back of my mind, I kept thinking, "It will all make sense in the book." But what fucking book? There was no book. There weren't even cohesive notes.

Back in the halfway house—great name—one of our assignments was to write down our story, and in the process, discover the problems. I can't remember what they called it, but at the time it was a very important part of the therapy. You just kind of started by saying, "I was born so-and-so, and my parents were so-and-so, and we lived in so-and-so." And this was a big deal. Everybody took it seriously. It was a perfect excuse to start "the book." But, of course, that didn't happen.

What did happen is that everyone was very protective of their little notebooks, because what the counselors wanted was more of a show-and-tell of all your sins, fuck-ups, and incidences of bad luck. So, as everybody got into it and started listing the gory details of their private lives, the relief factor was tremendous, but so was the paranoia. What if somebody were to get their hands on this and read it? Oh my God, the public confessional, everyone would know. . . . It was everyone's secret worry.

Fate has a way of confirming your paranoia, either by making a joke out of it, or allowing the worst to happen and giving you, in your last moments, the chance to say, "I knew it, I just fucking knew it."

I kept my notebook under my mattress and always kept my bed perfectly made. One day, as part of my "trustee" status, I was assigned to a work detail in the basement. If we could clean out a couple of the basement rooms, admin thought, we could move the junk out of some of the upstairs bedrooms and make space for about eight more "clients."

As it turned out, one of the rooms in the basement was three feet deep in old notebooks. When I informed the housemother—or should I say, grandmother?—she took it pretty calmly. "Oh, those. Yes, everybody leaves them under their mattress."

So it all ends up in somebody's basement. All your deep, dark secrets you've worried about all your life, afraid that someone might find out. Now, the only question was do we burn them, or just put them in garbage bags? But what if the garbage men read them? Yeah, they're such avid readers.

Just another reality flash. You can't tell all and kid yourself that someone will be interested. The drying out process is really the crying out process, and then coming to grips with the fact that no one wants to hear. So I needed to keep it grainy, just tell little stories, stop bogging down in strange conclusions.

Patrick always said that you couldn't talk about being high because it just didn't work. Talking about being straight was even more ho-hum. So maybe I could concentrate on sleep, I thought, or a self-help book like, *How to Take Lots of Drugs and Not Get Bored Going to Malls and Watching TV.*

But there was no dreamy, lofty consistency. I'd get up each day and try to start a better book than I'd started the day before. It usually worked out to a couple of pages. Sometimes it was in direct reaction to what I heard on the TV, read in the paper, or heard on the radio. Then it dawned on me that when I lived in Europe, I'd write about or shoot pictures of what I saw, what was actually there, basically because I didn't understand too much of what was in the paper and on the radio.

So, there I was, now a sort of video puppet. The robot spoke, I reacted. And I wondered why my life was empty and confusing. What I thought were my deepest personal problems were actually bundles of confusion I absorbed from the corporate media. I'd digest the media spew, and then, in a day or two, this big, mysterious, deep-seated problem would emerge. What a bunch of shit. I wondered if I could do something about it . . . so much to talk about; nothing to say.

So the editing process stretched out ahead of me. I wondered what embarrassing piece of writing or horrible photo would be posthumously published and held up for the world to crow about. "See, this guy was just an asshole who, even though slightly deranged, couldn't spell, and suffered from no education and too many drugs."

CHAPTER THIRTY-EIGHT

Love and War

Trying to make a whole lot of sense out of things that didn't make all that much sense at the time was frustrating, and I was getting the feeling it was also pretty useless.

One day, as I struggled for the words to come, I talked to a guy on the phone whose story of a lifetime ago sounded like the one I'd known. His everyday reality couldn't have been more different than mine: he was probably in his thirties or early forties, ran his dad's trucking company, was thinking of investing in another business, and seemed easygoing and generally well-adjusted. But he used to be "somewhat of a radical," he told me.

"Let's see," he said, "it must've been '70 or '71. I had hair down to my waist. I went to see a Rod Stewart concert down at the municipal auditorium. I'd never really been to a concert before. I mean, I'd seen bands in bars, that kind of thing, but this was my first real concert. I got really stoned and just went. I walked in about the time the lights dimmed and the Faces jumped out onstage. They were great. I'd never seen anything like it.

"After the show, I walked around the auditorium and just walked right in the back door. Nobody said a word or tried to stop me. I guess it was my long hair; they must've thought I was somebody, because nobody said a thing. I walked up to Stewart and started talking to him. He was a great guy.

"My life changed that night," he remembered. "I don't know what it was, really, but I was never the same. I took the money I'd saved for college, grabbed my girlfriend and went to southern Mexico, the jungle, man. We stayed there two years, then headed for Afghanistan. We got as far as Jamaica before my lights started to dim. You know what I mean?"

Did I know what he meant? Hey, I told him, not only do I know what you

Rod Stewart
1974

mean, but I taped that concert you went to and shot about ten rolls of film, left with the band, and wound up in France with a hangover.

So there we were, two strangers on the phone exchanging fundamentals, but what we were really talking about, neither one of us knew. Was it just normal life with a few drugs thrown in? Or was it a magic unfolding of human spirituality that, once experienced, one could no longer express, but only reminisce about with someone who'd at one time felt the same thing, too?

Something like world war was so much easier to describe: Well, the Germans came, and then we started dropping bombs, and then so on and so on. But what this magic spell was, no one could seem to put their finger on. And when you can't put your finger on something, you can't be specific, and therefore, you're vague. And if you're vague, well, then it must not have meant all that much in the first place, and, more than likely, you blew a few fuses in the process. Or so they'd have us believe.

Fact was, and still is, the magic was bewildering to those who didn't see it and overwhelming for those who did. And for a few short years, things were so simplified that it was a case of you either got high or you didn't. Music promoters and radio station owners were the first to feel the crunch. The number of people who got high was growing by leaps and bounds, and they wouldn't listen to music that was made by people who didn't get high, who didn't know what was happening. They could tell in seconds if the music was high or not, even though it was radically different within each clique. I mean, to someone who didn't get high, what did James Taylor have in common with Jimi Hendrix? Why would one promoter in Cleveland lose his shirt on "Direct from England! Freddy and the Dreamers!" while an albino from Beaumont, Texas, would pull in thousands of kids at twice the price?

To the outsider, it was baffling. And bafflement turned to hate.

Ron Wood
Faces tour, 1975

CHAPTER THIRTY-NINE

Roadies

Today, they're guitar techs, back liners, and sound engineers, but these guys usually started out as band helpers, and if they stuck with it, they became roadies. Today it's almost a derogatory term. But from the mid-'60s to the mid-'80s, "roadie" meant something special.

Top-drawer roadies were almost like stealth band members. The audience never saw them until the houselights went on. For the Stones, it was Stu, who was so good he actually played keyboards onstage and in the studio with the band. He was a big guy and looked more like a well-fed American football player than one of the Stones. Stu was a great piano player, but knew he didn't look the part, so he handled the equipment, waiting 'til the last minute to sit down at the piano off to the side of the stage. He wasn't a big drug connoisseur; in fact, he was prone to pack everything up after a show, go back to the hotel and crash, leap out of bed at the crack of dawn, and go play golf somewhere until noon—about the time the Stones would be getting their first wake-up call. Keith Richards claimed Stu knew more about music—blues, especially—than all the Stones put together.

Harry Tibitts, who worked for Traffic, was the roadie's roadie. There was nothing humble about his approach to heavy lifting. Harry was cool—he talked cool, acted cool, looked cool, and dressed like he had a back door to Hendrix's closet with his hats, silk scarves, and tailor-made leather jackets. Those who didn't know better instantly assumed that he was probably Traffic's lead singer or guitar player. Like most roadies, Harry could play guitar, but he was the first one to dress like a superstar all the time. Because of Harry, roadies' perceptions of themselves were forever changed—they could be stars, too.

Stu and Harry both died early on, but they were what roadies were all about. Roadies were so much more than heavy equipment movers. They

Harry Tibitts
Traffic roadie, 1967

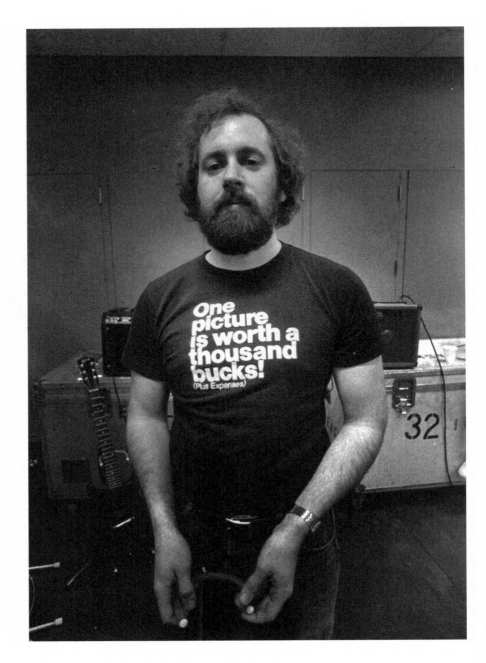

Eagles roadie
Long Run tour

were the ground troops that held the band together. And though it wasn't Stu's thing, roadies typically outdrank and outpartied the guys they worked for, plus stayed up later, bagged more women, fought better, and were just as proficient at their instruments. After Harry Tibitts showed up, they even began to look like stars, sort of; it's hard to keep up a fabulous wardrobe when you're unloading trucks in the alley and dragging gear onstage.

Bob Pridden has been with the Who since the beginning. Chuch Magee was with the Stones for twenty-five years and with Rod Stewart for seven years before that. These guys were selfless. They lived for the band and to give the band's fans the best possible show. While the band stayed up all night and crashed all day to "rest up for the gig," it was the roadies who went down to the hall, set up the stage and the gear, waited for soundcheck, and made the show happen. Roadies were a breed apart. They did ten times the work of the band, for none of the glory and very little of the money.

Today, it's different, and it's nobody's fault. There's so much equipment, it's so high-tech, so refined, so damn complicated and nonpersonal. Everyone's a specialist, a technician, an engineer. Just as the neighborhood mechanic's been replaced by a kid with a clipboard who hooks a computer scanner to your engine, true roadies have grown up or died, replaced by guys with digital guitar tuners.

Mark Patterson, James Gang roadie
Goose Lake, 1970

Back when the Who were being called the loudest band in the world, all their sound gear could be packed in the luggage bins at the bottom of the Greyhound. A recent Stones tour saw sixty-five semis full of sound gear, plus two generator trucks that supplied power to the stage. And that was only half of it. While the band played in St. Louis, the same amount of trucks was in Chicago, setting up for the next night. Crew A and crew B.

I remember John Sinclair at the Grande one afternoon, after delivering some MC5 posters. He picked up the newspaper and read aloud that the Beatles weren't gonna tour anymore because the crowds were getting too big and nobody could hear. "With the money these assholes make, they could put a speaker in everybody's lap," Sinclair quipped. No doubt. Technology continued to keep pace with the concert tour until it was something huge, something colossal . . . sixty-five semis full, and then some.

*Firefall roadie
Miami, mid-'70s*

James Gang roadie Mark Patterson

Faces roadies
1974

Bill Robbins, Bob Seger's roadie
1973

CHAPTER FORTY

Who Again

In the late 1980s, my mom called the photography department of the University of Texas on my behalf and set up a meeting with the head curator, Roy Flukinger. She went with me as I carried in an armload of photos, a cross-section of what I considered my very best work. Roy seemed to like the shots, but I wasn't sure. When he'd gone through the whole stack, Roy announced that he—meaning the school—wanted my collection. Not just this armload of pictures. They wanted everything. I was stunned. There was one problem: the school would need an appraisal to determine the value of the entire collection—negatives, slides, prints, correspondence, writings, tapes. Roy had his secretary type up a list of qualified appraisers. We'd speak again after an official appraisal, he told me.

Roy's list included guys in New York, D.C., California, and one in Texas. Austin, in fact. John Payne. I gave John a call, and he agreed to come down to San Antonio and look at what I had, all spread out in my studio. This was the free estimate. The real appraisal he thought he could do in less than two days at a fee of $500 per hour. He left; I went into shock. John eventually offered me a deal, basically a senior citizen's discount, so I borrowed some money and had an appraisal done. Within a week we had an IRS-legal appraisal, and what would become an eight-year acquisition process began.

The main reason for the delay was a single, seemingly simple question: since a lot of the pictures were of famous people, did the stars in the photos have some claim upon their use? The University turned the question over to their law school. The issue was debated, and after four years the conclusion was finally returned that the collection was a body of work that, in its entirety, was a work of art, and therefore, 100 percent Property of the Artist.

In 1989, I got a call from Chris Easter. He was living in Austin, going to college, and dating the daughter of my appraisal guy, John Payne. We'd never met.

Pete Townshend

on L.A. soundstage between takes of promo film Call Me Lightning, 1968

The Who had just announced the launch of their "The Kids Are Alright" tour, commemorating twenty-five years as a band and twenty years since *Tommy*'s debut. Chris was a huge Who fan, probably the most enthusiastic I've ever met. He'd asked John if that Who photographer John had appraised was going on the tour. John said he didn't know, but he gave him my phone number and encouraged him to call me in San Antonio.

I had a small studio in a warehouse there, where I was drinking about a quart of vodka a day, washing it down with lots of cold Mexican beer, and drinking wine at night with a couple of old flames who'd come to the studio after dark to get decadent. Chris called about ten one night. I was slurring

Who crowd
Tampa, Florida, 1989

everything. I told him that I'd heard about the Who thing, but I was out of that now and didn't have the funds or the urge to go. He started working on me. He told me that I owed it to history to shoot the band. This would be the last tour, an important chapter in my story. He went on and on, and finally asked if he could drive down to San Antonio to talk about it. The next day, he showed up with an airplane ticket to Toronto, the first gig, and a thousand dollars in cash. "You've got to go," he told me.

I told him that there was no way I could repay him; I'd been falling-down drunk for months. He told me to think about it, that I didn't need to pay him back. All he wanted was to meet Pete when the Who came to Texas in a few weeks. If I'd at least try to make that happen, he'd call it even.

The plane ticket was for the next morning, the day of the show in Toronto. I grabbed a few cameras and some clothes and headed for the airport.

Who tour
1989

By two that afternoon, after a $60 cab ride from the airport, I found myself at the backstage fence. Guys on the other side were half my age, all suntanned and wearing tour shirts. Eventually, some kid came over. I gave him my name, and he said he'd ask around the production office if anyone knew who I was. He returned in two minutes with a fat envelope with my name on it. Inside were an all-access pass, itinerary tour book, and list of all the accommodations on the tour.

I wandered around the giant football stadium watching the crew hang banks of lights and massive video screens. This was gonna be a huge production. I got some sandwiches, sat out in the sea of empty folding chairs, and fiddled with my cameras until the band showed up for soundcheck.

When Pete looked out and saw me, he ran down from the stage and onto the field. We hadn't seen each other in years.

"I hoped you would come!" Pete told me. "We didn't know where you were. We'll ride back to the hotel together. Barney is here and he brought his son Fred along. This is gonna be fun.

"Check out this drummer, Simon Phillips," Pete went on excitedly. "We have singers, another guitar player, a horn section. We all brought our kids— so far they love being over here."

Big stadiums, big crowds, big money. I wound up traveling with the band for the entire tour, which included full-length performances of *Tommy* in Los Angeles and New York.

Nearly three months and forty dates later in Dallas, I introduced Chris to Pete and took a picture of them together. That photo is now matted and framed and hangs above Chris's fireplace in Austin. Chris and I talked every

Who tour
How many limos does it take to move a quarreling four-piece band?
1982

Mandy Moon, Keith's daughter with the Who, 1989

few months after that, and he was solid encouragement. In 2003, when I had my show in Michigan, he put up the money to have my catalog published. After the Who Convention in April 2006, as I was filling Chris in on all the details, including the fact that the band was going to tour again in Europe, he floored me again with another irresistible offer.

"Take me as your assistant and I'll pay for it. You won't have to spend a dime." So Chris picked up the tab for the trip to Switzerland—lock, stock, and Eurail passes—and was the best assistant I've ever had. When we'd made it back from the "Who's Left" tour, I invited him to join me in Los Angeles for the James Gang rehearsals. The Gang had paid for my ticket and hotel room, so Chris met me in L.A. and wound up running errands, carrying cameras, and shadowing me as I took photos. We had a blast.

It took eight years, but I've managed to pay Chris back for the Toronto ticket. In Europe, I got him on stage twice, ten feet away from Townshend, a lifetime dream of his. He finally got his money back from the catalog last year, and he used frequent flyer miles to get to L.A. He said it was the best summer of his life.

CHAPTER FORTY-ONE

Amazing Grace

2002. I'd just driven my mom to Tampa to see family and attend my son's martial arts school demonstration at a big mall in Clearwater. When the phone rang, I was sure it was Tim calling with directions to the restaurant for dinner, but it was Russ Schlagbaum. He'd been working with the Stones and was calling from Toronto, where the band was in rehearsals for their upcoming tour.

"It's Chuch," Russ said. He spoke in a monotone, his words deliberate. I knew instantly something was wrong.

"He died. He collapsed right after lunch break. They stretched him out on some guitar cases and Johnny Starbuck tried to revive him, and when he couldn't, he just kept pounding on his chest and yelling. The roadies had to pull him off. He was dead on arrival at the hospital."

At first, I couldn't even remember the last time I'd seen Chuch. Then I recalled that one time he and his wife, Claire, had driven down in the snow and spent the night. Chuch had said a blessing before dinner. I'd kept my eyes open. In all the years I'd known him, he'd never said a blessing at the dinner table before. As he prayed, he'd almost burst into tears, he was so grateful for everything. This, I'd thought, was the grown-up Chuch, and it was good to see, somehow.

It'd been quick, according to Russ, a massive heart attack. The band had immediately stopped rehearsals. Claire had told them that Chuch did not wish to be embalmed, which, in Michigan, meant the remains must be buried within thirty-six hours. So the entire Rolling Stones tour machine was now pulling every string they could find to get Chuch back to Marquette, way up in Michigan's Upper Peninsula, where he had lived the past fifteen years between tours.

I had two days to make it from Florida to Michigan. Mom and I needed to leave right then. It was already after dark. We drove straight through,

Chuch Magee
Rolling Stones tour, 1976

stopped at the house in Central Lake long enough to pick up funeral clothes and shower, and kept going until we got to Marquette. The Stones chartered a plane and brought most of their entourage right into downtown Marquette, Michigan.

Not many knew that Chuch had been a longtime churchgoer. In his church, at the altar under the sixty-foot cathedral ceiling, an easel held a large color photo of Chuch, matted and framed. It was a shot of him taken on the last tour, backstage in Dallas. He was standing in front of Keith's guitars, at least twenty of them, all lined up like they were hanging in a closet. He was smiling. Chuch almost never smiled, even when he laughed. But in that photo, you knew that every guitar was perfectly tuned and ready to go, and you could feel that at that moment, he had fulfilled his very destiny.

The church was packed; people standing in the side aisles, the balcony filled, the choir stands shoehorned with the troubled children Chuch and the church had helped. Over the years, he had taken these problem kids and taught them how to plant cedars. They'd planted thousands of trees, and Chuch had rescued hundreds of kids headed for trouble.

The Stones filed down the middle aisle and, one at a time, hugged Chuch's wife of twenty years, then settled in the second pew. No one said a word. The Stones looked distinguished, low-key, and stunned into earthliness. Chuch was younger than anyone in the band. One minute he was here; the next, he was gone.

A woman from the church told several stories about Chuch and all the children he'd helped—the difference between college and jail for many of them. A church trio played some gospel songs, and then a young preacher spoke. He eulogized Chuch in the most uplifting way, speaking of how he got juvenile delinquents to care about the environment, to start thinking, to take positive action. He spoke about Chuch's work with the Rolling Stones, the influence that he had on the crew, and his value to the band. The preacher had called all the family and friends he could find; every one of them had told him another story of Chuch's decades with Ron Wood, how he'd been brought in as Ronnie's guitar guy, but did stuff for everybody, how he was a lifer.

The preacher was right. Roadies and crew always came and went. Maybe they'd go out for one tour then you'd never hear from them again. But Chuch, he was always there. If you needed to know something quick, you'd ask Chuch. If you needed the impossible, just tell Chuch. Yet, out of a hundred or so in the crew, Chuch was the only guy that Mick Jagger could not order around. Chuch's job description: he's Woody's guy. This seemed to annoy Mick for the first ten years or so. After a while, though, he was just a part of everything. Recording in the Caribbean, rehearsing in Canada, touring Brazil, Chuch was there—and Mick eventually accepted it.

After a prayer, Ron, Keith, and Mick filed to the front—Charlie stayed seated—and picked up guitars. A bassist appeared in the corner of the choir section with an upright bass. Ron sat down, a Dobro slide guitar in his lap. Keith had an amplified acoustic. Mick stood behind the mic and pulled a harmonica from his shirt pocket. And it began.

The sound filled the church. The guitars came through the sound system so clear, so strong, you felt as though your head was inside the instrument. The notes were delicate and familiar, "Amazing Grace." It was the most celestial music I'd ever heard. When Mick came in on harmonica, it was the wail and moan in everyone's heart. Tears streamed down Keith's face as he stared up at the ceiling, playing the most poignant blues guitar you could imagine. It was the best thing the band had ever played, a declaration of love and talent, given in tribute to a life given.

The band returned to their seats as the last notes resonated throughout the sanctuary. No one made a sound. We all sat motionless until the last strains faded into silence. Not one person clapped. Everyone cried.

Slowly, people rose and exited the church, wiping tears from their eyes.

Chuch Magee, Ron Wood, and Keith Richards the day after the bust Toronto, 1977

Heart Attack

CHAPTER FORTY-TWO

I was calm in the ambulance, the medics monitoring my pulse and firing off a steady barrage of questions to keep me conscious. I wasn't in pain. I could feel that our driver was good—aggressive, but not jerky—and we were hauling ass. I wasn't worried about an ambulance crash. I looked around at all of the equipment, the metal doors, the oxygen tanks, all squeaky-clean and looking efficient. I knew I was in good hands. These guys were focused, and I could hear from the two-way radio that the hospital was expecting me.

It wasn't easy to take inventory of my life while talking steadily to the medic, at his insistence. But I did.

Mom—wonderful.
Dad—wonderful.
Son—wonderful.
Wife—wonderful.
Family—wonderful.
Friends—wonderful.
Places I've been—wonderful.
Phenomenal music I've heard—wonderful.

I felt so privileged, so grateful to have witnessed the wonder of things in this life. I couldn't have imagined more. My demons, if they'd ever existed, were at bay; I wasn't riding along craving a bottle of vodka. There in that ambulance, I wasn't feeling, *Okay, this is serious, time to start thinking differently.* No, it was more like, *It's been this serious all along.* And now my life was in the hands of people who knew what they were doing. I was at peace. A totally grateful peace.

Even the hard stuff, the painful stuff—profound struggles, deep sadness,

Who tour
Dallas, 1975

true free-world poverty—were privileges to have experienced. All I could think of as the medics rolled me through the emergency entrance and onto a hospital gurney was that this was a wonderful life.

I take full responsibility. The depression, the mayhem, the confusion—mine and those I've caused others—were entirely self-inflicted.

My whole human experience had centered around smoking pot and drinking alcohol. The family seemed largely in the background. But it had just seemed totally normal, every step of the way.

Under my first stepfather's rule, I could drink at home: a beer at lunch, a glass of wine sometimes with dinner. At sixteen, when I moved with the family to London, I could go to the fridge and have a beer at any time. I could drink outside of the house, as well; in England you're legal at fifteen or sixteen.

Then there was school. Art school life *was* pub life. The move to Paris found me switching over to red wine, which you could get in cafés 24-7, and cheap. On Ibiza, wine was thirty-five pesetas a liter, under thirty cents. Cigarettes were ten pesetas a pack, about seven cents. You could buy *Benzadrina* tablets at the *farmacia* for a penny apiece, if you bought fifty at a time.

Drinking was something that happened every day on Ibiza. People who weren't drinking were sick or under the weather. The peasant farmers sipped their morning coffee with cognac, enjoyed wine with lunch and dinner. There was no Diet Coke, no milk, no other options, because there was no fridge. If you were a kid, you got sweet, room-temperature tea.

I considered myself a good drinker. I didn't wobble, get rowdy, throw up, or slur my words too much. I liked drinking all the time and it didn't seem to bother me. Others would eventually want to crash out, dry out, at least for a few hours. Not me.

To imagine my life in England, France, and Spain without drinking is impossible. It made everything else bearable. It brought meaning, brought fun to life.

Just as it would wreak havoc with it later.

After decades of drinking, I created some deep, dark problems. Like discovering that I couldn't just quit, for one. So I pretended that it wasn't a problem, kept doing it and trying to cover it up. I created my own nightmare. Alcohol, above and beyond everything else, is a depressant, and after twenty years of ingesting depressants, you wind up pretty damn depressed—even if it looks like you should be having fun. I was never violent, nor did I become a thief. I just drank 'til I passed out. Then I'd wake up and do it all over again.

So I take responsibility.

But I don't apologize.

It happened; it was a pivotal part of my life. I cannot take it back.

It's not like Johnny Cash saying, "Yeah, I took a lot of speed and drank a lot of bourbon and wrote a lot of hit songs and now that I'm a millionaire, I'm sorry." John, if you hadn't taken that speed and drank all that booze, you wouldn't have written anything. You'd have been a sales manager at Sears. You got what you prayed for, so shut the hell up.

I prayed, too, on occasion. Not for goodies or handouts, but for direction, guidance. I'd ask, "What do you want me to do?" And it was always frightening, simply because the answer was always instantaneous.

It started with the first prayer I can really remember. 1959. It was back in Florida, on Eddie Thompson's back porch. I was sitting with my guitar on my lap, trying to play the Jimmy Reed bouncing shuffle progression—all three movements, E to A to B, and then back to E again—yet still maintain some sort of rhythm. My fingers were blistered and sore and I can remember squeezing my eyes closed and asking God in whispers to please let me play that, and if I could play that, I wouldn't ask for anything else. As far as the guitar was concerned, I would be satisfied.

Nearly thirty years later, standing in the Super S grocery in Divine, Texas, it dawned on me: I could play the Jimmy Reed riffs, all of them, and that was all I ever learned to play. I got, in other words, exactly what I asked for. I was overwhelmed. I'd prayed to stay out of the Army during Vietnam. I'd prayed to marry Mary Ann. Prayer worked.

I was so blown away by the realization, I didn't know what to do. Should I pray for bigger and better things? Should I save it for the really major stuff? Should I launch into a testimonial right there in the Super S, fall down on my knees, or work my way calmly to the cashier and wish her a nice day?

The frightening part of prayer, I realized back then and believe to this day, is that it works. That's why I don't do it anymore. It's the response. It's so sudden, so clear—it scares me.

So when I was dying and had my chest cut open, I wasn't praying to live longer.

I was simply saying, "Thank you. I lived and learned so much."

Roof inspection
day before Goose Lake Festival
Michigan, 1970

Walsh Says It's My Destiny

CHAPTER FORTY-THREE

From: Ronnie Wood
Sent: Sunday, October 30, 2005
To: Tom Wright
Subject: RE: Tom Wright Update

Tom,

We don't have time to come in to perform "Amazing Grace" for you.
We love you dearly and I will let the rest of the boys know.

Ronnie

From: Pete Townshend
Sent: Sunday, October 30, 2005
To: Tom Wright
Subject: RE: Tom Wright Update

Tom,

Hard to believe the living anxiety attack has had a heart anxiety episode.
You have so much to live for still, so much work still to do. Your irregular
missives to me still shape my life and often harden me up—there are
few others I care to listen to, but I will always listen to you. We are all
totally committed to you whatever your decision, but obviously, selfishly,
we would like you to do the bypass. I know dozens of guys who've had
this; once it's done their lives seem to crash on as before but with a
better diet!

Pete

Joe Walsh
James Gang Rides Again shoot

From: Ian McLagan
Sent: Sunday, October 30, 2005
To: Tom Wright
Subject: RE: Tom Wright Update

Tom,

Stop fucking about and get well!

But seriously, you have our Big Love and hugs and health and long life
please. We'll be thinking of you constantly and want you to get better
very soon.

Our hearts go out to yours, you know?

Love,

Mac

From: Wayne Kramer
Sent: Saturday, October 29, 2005
To: Tom Wright
Subject: RE: Tom Wright Update

Tom, as I'm sure you're aware, there are way better ways to get old
friends to check in. You are in my prayers.

Love and respect,

Wayne Kramer

From: Pete Townshend
Sent: Tuesday, November 01, 2005
To: Tom Wright
Subject: Another message from Pete

Ha! Sanity prevails. What great news. God, I wish I wasn't so busy, I long
to come and clean out your arteries myself. What is great about this
is that it has made me aware I too must be more careful about what I
eat. When you hit sixty, you have bypassed a lot of burgers and fries let
alone hearts.

Pete

From: Pete Townshend
Sent: Saturday, November 05, 2005
To: Tom Wright
Subject: From Pete

Dear Tom,

Seven bypasses, you're the man of rock. I was thinking about you when I got the news about your heart trouble. I was watching the Dylan documentary, the part where he steals albums from the house of a friend, and goes off to study them. If I hadn't met you, I wouldn't have had that same kind of education. How the hell did you manage to know what to listen to, where to find it, and establish such incredible criteria so early in your life?

I'm so happy you have recovered.

Love

Pete

Walsh says it's my destiny. "Yeah, man, that's the only reason you're still alive—it's to finish that book."

He ought to know; he offered to foot my whole $100,000 medical tab. Of course, I turned him down. But the gesture meant more than I can say.

Walsh called the other day from soundcheck down at Pine Knob, outside of Detroit. For some reason, Smokey decided from my email that I was too ill to make the trip, so Joe called to make sure I was okay.

He understood why I wasn't there for that James Gang reunion show and was proud of me for not losing writing time, which would've been the case had I driven down and hung out, no doubt for a day or three. The Gang loved the pictures I'd shot at the L.A. rehearsals, he said. The session made them feel like a band again. And in the photos, they looked like a band, a solid one, older, but not burnt out. Healthy, determined. Cool.

The rehearsals had been a million miles away from the James Gang, round one, circa 1969. In L.A., the band was set up according to a sketch. The instruments and amps were mic'd before the band ever got there. There was a guy on the right hand side of the stage mixing the floor monitor system, and the soundboard was twelve feet long with billions of knobs. Both the monitor tech and the mixing board belonged to the Eagles. The board was pulling light duty with the James Gang—just three band members, an organ player, and a trio of backup singers.

From the first note, the sound was sliced and diced, everything separated, just the way the Eagles liked it. But the James Gang, they're a bar band and always have been, and that's a one-sound thing. Everything should mesh and interweave. The drums and bass should surround the guitar and support everything so that even if the guitar stops, you still know it's there and the music keeps pumping to that bump-grind-drink bar band beat. At

Joe Walsh on chopper
before Rides Again shoot
New England

the rehearsals, the sound never blended together. It'd probably work itself out on the road, I thought.

When he called, Joe said the band had really come together, the shows were sold out, the crowds were amazing. But he told me again that I did the right thing to stay home and write. The book was more important. I knew Joe was right.

Joe always calls it like he sees it. Like when CD players first came out. We were sitting on the Eagles' old turboprop tour plane somewhere over Texas; somebody had a portable CD player, and they were talking about how clear and clean everything was. Walsh's only comment: "I miss the hiss." Like gum on my shoe, that's stayed with me ever since. Plus, who could forget Joe's 1973 album title, *The Smoker You Drink, the Player You Get?* Talk about summing up the intermission of the rock renaissance.

When he's playing with the Eagles, Walsh is the colorful sidekick, the raw rocker in an otherwise fairly mellow band. But he's still the new guy. With the James Gang, he's the chief and leader, Mister Responsibility. Music director and choir coach. In the early days, he'd have to sell his ideas to everyone. Now, the sheer clout of his résumé gives him full authority. Still, Joe's trying to discover while leading. These days, he's after the profound like a bloodhound on a scent.

When I went to L.A. for their rehearsals, I'd just returned from the Who shows in Switzerland and Austria and brought a bunch of those shots with me to L.A., including one of Pete as we met in Austria, one of Roger cutting my hair, one of the engine of the Lufthansa airbus as I was walking up the ramp, my favorite.

"How's Pete?" Joe asked when he saw the picture of Townshend. Before I could answer, Joe said, "I don't think he likes me anymore. He's so moody, and so am I. Maybe we're just getting cranky. Or maybe it's because the Eagles are so successful—"

I interrupted Joe, saying I knew for a fact that any success Joe achieved made Pete happy for him, not jealous of him.

"Well, I gave him a guitar, a $20,000 guitar," Joe went on, "and he sold it on eBay."

Things went quiet.

"Roger's okay, he's a nice guy," Joe said after a few moments, looking at the photo of Daltrey. "And you've got to admit, Roger always sings Pete's words with conviction."

Pete would tell me later he sold a Flying V guitar Joe had given him in 1989 prior to the Who's big reunion tour. "I was broke," Pete said. "I'd been working as an editor at Faber & Faber for several years. Ironically, after the 1989 Who tour, I was a millionaire for the first time in my life. I tried to get the guitar back, but Alan Rogan had sold it secretly to a collector." Pete also sold his D'Angelico, and a Gretsch Merle Travis, both worth over $100,000 today. "But, hey," he said, "I kept the old Fender Bandmaster amplifier, and the orange Gretsch Country Gentleman, and the Edwards pedal that Joe gave me after I gave him an ARP 2600 synthesizer. He said it would make me sound like Neil Young. I used it on *Who's Next*, on 'Bargain,' and it made me sound like me." Pete used the exact same rig on the new Who CD, he said.

Back in L.A. with the James Gang, the pictures of the Who in Europe were so current they made me seem current, in spite of a gum infection that caused my face to almost double in size. It took four days of antibiotics before it finally deflated, like a tired, old balloon.

Dale kept telling me I didn't look any different. I'd find a mirror and stare at elephant man for a while, and then just give up worrying about it.

Walsh said, "It's okay, Tom, you can have a swollen face. It's okay."

My destiny—in L.A., at least.

Meanwhile, Back at the Grande

CHAPTER FORTY-FOUR

After I came out of heart surgery, Russ Gibb and I spoke on the phone. I hadn't seen him since the late '70s and the Grit Kids project. In '03, I'd invited him to come up to Traverse for my photo show. He couldn't make it, but at least we were back in touch.

When Russ called, I told him that I'd seen one of the Grit Kids recently in the grocery store near my home. The Kid, now forty-something, was visiting his parents-in-law. He was now as wide as he was tall, with a hermit beard, and I felt sorry for him. In his mind, he'd never left the Grit Kids. It was sad to think that as mentors we hadn't done more to add a little balance to the Kids' lives.

From: Tom Wright
Sent: Tuesday, December 06, 2005
To: Russ Gibb
Subject: late response

Hi Russ,

It's a little late to respond to your emails, but I have several excuses. Bypass rehab consists of long periods of boredom laced with waves of depression and panic. The PBS station didn't play the Cream reunion, but an expose of illegal Mexican maids in L.A., so I guess I'll have to buy the DVD. Thanks for the tip anyway. Also I got the MC5

Billy Preston
Chicago, mid-'70s

update. I guess they will be able to tour for the next few years as the 5. Wayne Kramer has been a likeable guy all along, so I am happy for him.

I don't know how you have managed on the health front, or if you have had any close calls, but I can tell you I feel like I was given quite a gift. Kind of a second chance at doing something worthwhile. The question is what. That spirit that was churned up in the '60s seems to have been hijacked and swept under rugs, and now it is even difficult to remember what was so important.

As the industrial age creaks, sputters, and falls all around us and the young blast off into cyberspace, nothing makes sense without the music holding the culture in unison. It doesn't feel like a normal sequence, but rather a result of a military strategy to rot things from within.

Not to get bogged down, but since I have been given some overtime I feel duty-bound not to waste it. This country could pull itself together overnight. Hollywood could help. A series of movies could show people how things could be, could inspire people to want to change their lives right then and there. Could show how ancient knowledge and truths could blend with the ability to make machines and tools, how high tech could be another spoke in the wheel, instead of all these elements working or dying in opposition to each other.

For instance, there's a language teacher in Connecticut who teaches six languages at once. In the time it takes to teach someone Spanish, he can teach them another five languages at the same level.

In Korea, they have something called Chisenbop. It's a system of mathematical calculating where students use their knuckles to work out hugely complicated math problems, like the square root of a twenty-digit number, calculus, algebra, whatever. When they flew a bunch of Korean twelve-year-olds to New York to compete against students with calculators, the Koreans never lost.

Every year we wind up with another million recalled and worn out tires, and the big question is where they're going to burn them. In Arizona, an architect is constructing houses and buildings out of them. They're laid sideways like bricks. The houses don't need heat or A/C; they're soundproof, bulletproof, and can be any shape you choose.

To wait for things to just come together would take too long, but to do science-fiction movies that glorified future harmony, good projects, and good deeds, instead of monsters, diabolical tyrants, and exploding solar systems seems to me at least a worthwhile dream.

I learned at the Grande. When you played shitty music, you had crowd problems, violence, and building damage. When you cleaned things up, painted the building, and played good music, the crowd felt like they could fix the world.

Still beating,

Tom

From: Russ Gibb
Sent: Wednesday, December 07, 2005
To: Tom Wright
Subject: RE: late response

Tom,

Thanks for the "thinking," we sure need more of it in today's world.

Your name was mentioned by the local announcer of the Cream show. May I use part of your letter on my web blog site?

Cheers,

Russ

October 2006. Forty years since the Grande'd first opened its doors to rock and roll, and Detroit wanted to celebrate. The anniversary concert, well-hyped in the Detroit papers, featured Big Brother and the Holding Company, Arthur Brown, Canned Heat, and Third Power. All played the Grande back in the day. One of my photos of Russ Gibb made the commemorative poster, and I was lured to the show with free food and accommodations. They wanted me to speak.

It was a five-hour drive to the Royal Oak Theatre. On the way down, I kept thinking of things to say about the Grande, about Russ, about how the Grande had affected the course of pop music, and why.

Russ was there, seventy-five years old and looking it. Dave Miller too, the Grande announcer, still walking around with a snake. Plus a crowd of 1,000, the Grande faithful.

Seeing all those Grande people, and meeting the really successful ones, was amazing. But more than that I realized that they knew so little of what was really going on back in the Grande's heyday. Even Russ, the club's founder, didn't seem to grasp the big picture. The Michigan public thought it was a big deal that Russ booked a bunch of English bands to come play in Detroit—period. And it was. But what happened when the musicians arrived was so much more complex and interesting.

Russ had chosen the Grande as a venue because it was small, cheap, and in the worst neighborhood, meaning that no one would care if people were getting high and going to loud concerts. At first, no one knew that the Grande was acoustically perfect. It became quickly obvious, though, that the place was possibly the best sound venue in the world. And when you combined those priceless acoustics with the most intense audience anyone in the rock world had ever seen . . . well, the Grande's impact was felt worldwide, with the mass public none the wiser.

When bands performed at the Grande, they actually got better. They'd come in for a soundcheck in the afternoon and immediately feel the building working with them, with the music. Suddenly, things sounded so much better than in rehearsals or at other halls. At the Grande, the ante was upped, and at showtime the musicians would wind up playing better than they'd ever thought was possible. Until the Grande came along, for most bands the concept of the venue itself actually working in their favor hadn't even been thought of.

At the reunion, what surprised me most was that people weren't standing around talking about this show or that show way back when. They talked about how they went into this or that business because of what happened at the club. The Grande—school for entrepreneurs.

When I got to the mic, I rambled on about the building's acoustics and how the Grande was the Stradivarius of ballroom sound, a near-perfect design the architect was proud of back in 1929.

The only quote of mine in the newspaper the next morning was, "This is where *Spinal Tap* meets *Jurassic Park*."

Bob Seger
1967

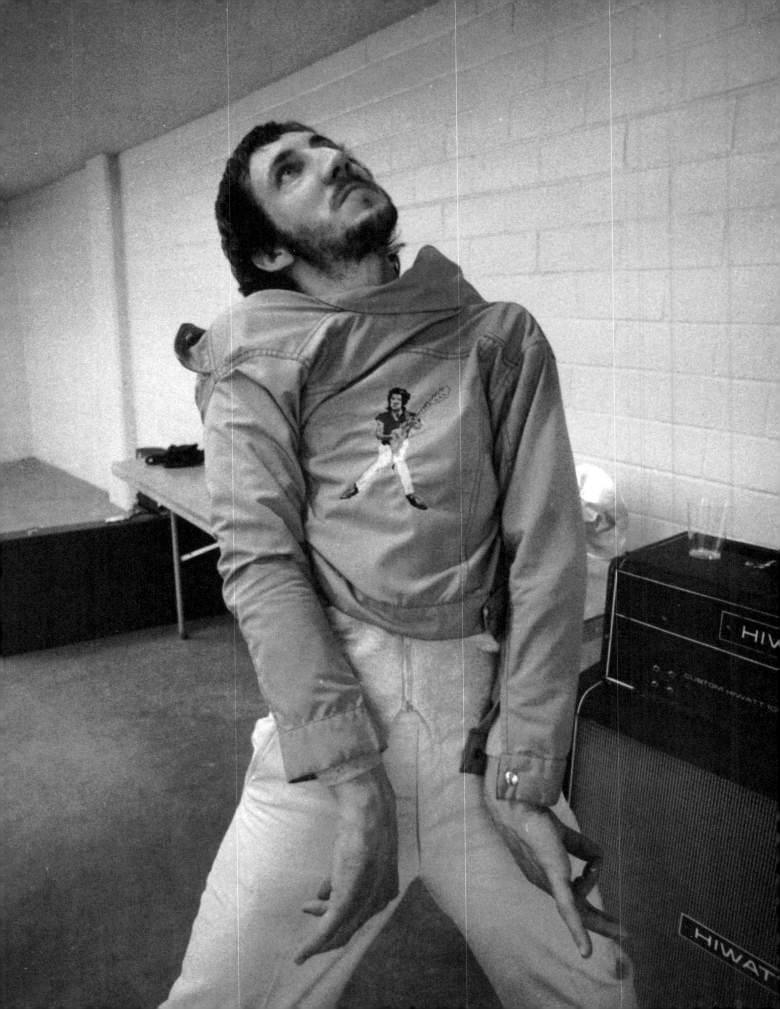

CHAPTER FORTY-FIVE

The New Who

2002. It was a late fall day in northern Michigan. Most leaves had turned tobacco brown and were now laying everywhere in big, wet wads. The reflection of the low clouds off the lake made everything double-gray. As I walked toward the post office, my cell phone rang. It was Roger Daltrey.

"Tom, it's Rodge. How are you?" He'd never called me. Ever.

"Are you in the States?" I asked him.

"No, I'm in England, mate. But I'm headed your way in a couple of days. I'm going to Montana to start filming a series for the History Channel. I got your letter, and I wanted to talk about it. You were all upset by the fact that Pete and I weren't even talking on the last tour. You said that we *had* to do a last album, a good-bye album, use new stuff that Pete and I would come up with in the studio, not even look in the box of unused Townshend songs."

I liked listening to Roger tell me what was in my letter.

"You said any studio in the world but Pete's. Just go in with notebooks and pencils. Pick a riff, build a pattern, make it cook then throw simple phrases in it. Work out some kick-ass, funky harmony instead of Pete singing high and old lady-ish, on his own, or me on my own, with the heavy metal bellow. You said put the voices together as much as possible. Make an album of short, simple songs that punch."

Obviously, Roger had read my letter to the end.

The post office was closed for lunch. I shivered as I paced the sidewalk out front. I couldn't remember ever getting a phone call from Roger in my

Pete Townshend
Houston, Texas
mid-'70s

life. This was important, I guessed. My letter apparently had some impact.

The note I sent to him was a quick summary of the one I'd sent to Townshend, the heavy one, with all the details. But Roger was getting charged up on the phone. If all the new stuff was Daltrey/Townshend, it would mean that Roger could get half of the song rights. If he and Pete could both go into a new studio together, instead of Roger being sent to the waiting area in Pete's house like a serf being dropped off to see the king—but hold on, the king is searching his files for some very heavy and moody songs that'd been vetoed thirty years before . . . well, it would be a whole, new Who.

"Tom, are you still there? Okay. Pete didn't want to talk this last tour. We played sad. But it didn't really bother me. The Pete you know is not the one I know. I know Pete from onstage. That's Pete to me, yeah, the real Pete. And that's plenty for me. Last tour, he was riveting and sharp as a bloody razor. I hope Pete and I can get together before I leave for the States. This TV thing is gonna go on for a couple of months."

Years later, Pete would tell me his side. That he felt Roger wanted to be seen as a songwriter, without actually being one. That it wasn't about half the money—though that was a part of it—but that it was really about Roger wanting a writer's dignity, something he's not had. And, sure, some bands do share songwriting royalties among the members who don't write, Pete would tell me, "But my father drummed it into me, over and over, that playing music, singing songs, will leave you poor—one day. But write the songs, and you will survive. It would be wrong for me to have taken that good advice, made enough money to buy my father a great car and his first house, and then pretend that in some way the magic was something I was sharing with a guy who trained his creative urges by cutting sheet metal."

Roger and I talked 'til my battery started beeping. He thanked me for the letter and said he'd call again. The lady in the post office unlocked the door and let me in. She was eating a sandwich and locked the door behind me.

"Thanks," I said absently, still dazed by the surprise call. "It was Roger Daltrey, phoning from London."

She took another bite of her sandwich.

The last Who tour raised as many questions as it sold tickets. People had come out of the bushes to see that 2002 tour. It'd started three days after John had died, locked in his room with a Las Vegas escort. He had cocaine in his system. John was being a bad boy. She had told a roadie in the hotel bar before they'd gone to the room that she was gonna "fuck him to death," or so that was the story from the road crew that'd been there. Roger'd said on the phone that John had always wanted to go out with a bang. Even so, it didn't seem right. Contracts and momentum made Pete and Rodge grab another bass player and hit the road. I caught the last couple of shows. The stage was full of musicians, but you couldn't help missing Keith Moon, and though John never moved when he played, his bass had been so orchestral that now, with a boom-boom-boom bass player and laid-back drummer, it was okay, but basically just hard-hitting sadness.

After the show in Toronto, Pete said he was glad it was finally all over. He said he wanted to go home and spend time with his son. There would be no more Who records, he said, and no more Who tours.

On the way back from Toronto, I couldn't stop thinking that Roger and Pete were like stepbrothers. Step twins, even. Arguing, fighting, playing, bad-mouthing each other for decades. I kept rolling words around in my head. Step Twins. "Once we were a group / Now we're a couple / In a band of brothers / Still joined at the buckle."

"Step Twins." How hard could it be? These guys *have* to make an album, I thought.

It would be bad manners not to.

CHAPTER FORTY-SIX

Fast Forward

From: Tom Wright
Sent: Wednesday, August 30, 2006
To: Pete Townshend
Subject: Question

Hi Pete,

Just ready to push the send button on some Hal Leonard catalog copy. It mentions my book will be published next year, and it says foreword by Pete Townshend, something I've taken for granted because I have the one you wrote back in '82, which is fine.

But in the back of my mind, I was hoping to ask you to write something longer, maybe the senior citizen's version, more of a grown-up reflection. I thought that would happen months from now, which is why I haven't asked you yet. Still, we have plenty of time to write something. The question is, are you okay with either the old one or an expanded version? And do you mind if I mention it to the publisher so it makes it in the catalog?

Tom

From: Pete Townshend
Sent: Wednesday, August 30, 2006
To: Tom Wright
Subject: Re: Question

Great news. I will happily expand my intro.

Pete

Pete Townshend
1967

Tom Wright. Good man. I have always been susceptible to a good man. . . .

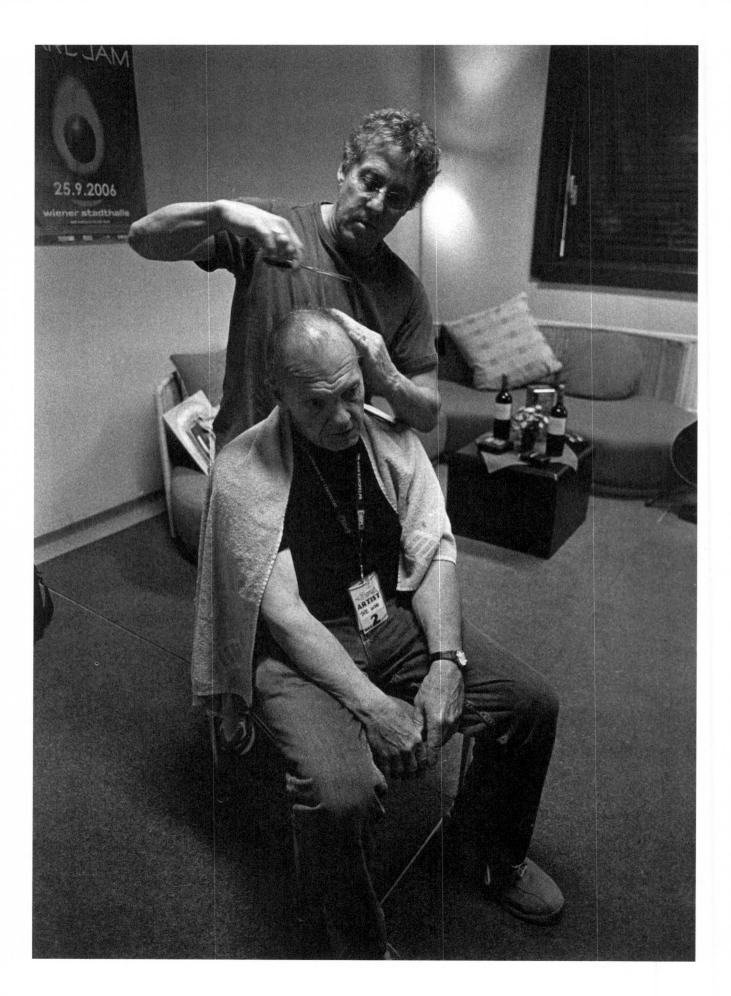

AUTHOR'S NOTE

Susan VanHecke was invited into this book project, and now I realize I couldn't have completed this without her. She painstakingly went through all of my old writings, and then drew new material from me by asking questions. Great questions. She worked so fast and so well it felt like she was inside my head. Then she took all these pieces and wove them into a verbal and visual tapestry. Without Sue, I'd still be stuck with boxes of notes that looked more like confetti than anything close to a tapestry. Sue made this happen. Now I can't imagine writing without her.

— Tom Wright

Hair Club for Men
Switzerland, 2006